A HEART FOR REFORMATION

A Heart for Reformation

C. Matthew McMahon

Puritan

PUBLICATIONS

ELGIN, ILLINOIS

www.puritanpublications.com

A Heart for Reformation
By C. Matthew McMahon
Copyright © 2007 by A Puritan's Mind

Published by Puritan Publications
A Ministry of A Puritan's Mind
834 Morgan Street
Elgin, IL 60123
www.puritanpublications.com

Layout & cover design: Matthew Steven Black

First Edition, 2007
Manufactured in the United States of America

Library of Congress Control Number: 2007925154

ISBN: 0-9765336-9-3

Dedicated to
all those that love the Lord Jesus Christ in sincerity.

And to my good brother in the Lord, Lance Maggiacomo, who
helped in editing the work for the good of the Kingdom of God

– we are expanding the Kingdom of God one book at a time.

Contents

There is nothing but filthiness and infection in us before God. For all the goodly virtues which we have to outward show, are but corruption till God have reformed us.

- *John Calvin, Sermons on Galatians*

Introduction

The purpose of this book is to set forth the nature of true
biblical reformation, and how that reformation should
permeate and extend to every sphere of the Christian's life.
Many times Christians will pick up books on "the Reformation"
hoping to read about William Tyndale, Martin Luther or John
Calvin. Those books are historical books on church history, and
how the great revival of the Reformation swept over the church
in God's providence for the good of recovering the Gospel
which had been hidden by the Roman Catholic Church. They
usually center on the hammering of Luther's *95 Theses* on the
door of the Wittenberg Church in 1517, and from there they begin to tell the story of how God providentially brought about
revival for the good of His church. But this book is not historical *perse*, rather, it is theologically practical. It is designed to
take the biblical principles of reformation, which were the practical out workings of the theology behind the Word of God, and
apply them to the contemporary church.

It is impossible to document history simply as chronological
events, but rather it is the intrusion of God into time to establish His redemptive purposes in and through men, and declare
His person and glory through the work of Jesus Christ. Two

epochs in God's work point to the greatest revolutions and revivals ever documented: the entrance of the Lord of Glory in the
fullness of time in the little town of Bethlehem, and the era of
the Reformation breaking out of a reign of eclipsing doctrinal
darkness and superstition. Christ brought forth the Gospel of
Jesus Christ, and the Reformers rescued the Gospel from
drowning in a sea of ecclesiastical expedience. But what should
Christians think concerning revival today? Is there room in the
present day for another "reformation"?

"Reformation" is defined by Webster's Dictionary as "a 16th
century religious movement marked ultimately by rejection or
modification of some Roman Catholic doctrine and practice
and establishment of the Protestant churches." That is the historical definition. There is another: "Reformation is the state of
being "reformed." Now one has to ask, from a biblical perspec-
tive, what this means. To be "reformed" or to "reform" means,
"1a) to put or change into an improved form or condition 1b) to
amend or improve by change of form or removal of faults or
abuses 2) to put an end to an evil by enforcing or introducing a
better method or course of action, 3) to induce or cause to abandon evil ways." Reformation, then, confronts and changes
the *status quo* in order to improve, amend, and introduce a better method of procedure. It removes, puts an end to, and abandons false or evil ways that hinder that which should already be
in place. In terms of *the* Reformation, it is the abandonment
and repudiation of the evil or wicked devices of men instituted
in the church through false doctrines, and to establish, change,
and amend those ways by immediate interposition of improved
change to the foundations of ecclesiastical truth found in Scripture. Such a term as "reformed", then, has some very important biblical connotations as well as historical connotations that
must be embraced. The importance, here, in the task of this
short book is a formal return to sound doctrine and truth previ-

ously eclipsed. It asks and answers the question, "Do *you* have a heart for reformation?"

The Reformers had hearts for Christ with the purpose of becoming reformed in their own thinking and reforming God's church for His glory. John Calvin poured many hours into writing various polemical works for the church that described and outlined how reformation should take place under varying circumstances. One of these works is called, *The Necessity of Reforming the Church*. It answers the following inquiry, "The question is not, whether the Church labors under diseases both numerous and grievous, (this is admitted even by all moderate judges,) but whether the diseases are of a kind the cure of which admits not of longer delay, and as to which, therefore, it is neither useful nor becoming to await the result of slow remedies. We are accused of rash and impious innovation, for having ventured to propose any change at all on the former state of the Church." Calvin wrote this tract while a Diet (a council) was taking place in the city of Spires, and desired to present it at the Diet in hopes of *further* reformation. The work covers three aspects of Reformation, 1) the evils which compelled the reformers to seek for remedies; 2) That the particular remedies which the Reformers employed were apt and salutary; and 3) That the reformers were not at liberty any longer to delay putting forth our hand, in as much as the matter demanded instant amendment. Calvin and the other Swiss reformers had been branded as working too quickly for Reformation. But Calvin replies in saying that they had not done anything too hastily, or rashly, desiring to show the necessity of their reforms over and against the intolerableness of a gradual reformation. Theodore Beza, one of Calvin's lifelong friends at Reformation, says of the work, "I know not if any writing on the subject, more nervous or solid, has been published in our age."

The matters which Calvin disputed in this tract on reforming the Church are 1) the cloak of evil hiding the head doctrines
of the Christian faith, 2) the neglect of the pure worship of God,
3) the sacraments being polluted and administered amiss, and
4) the government of the church being corrupted by "insuffer-
able tyranny." The biblical foundations of Christianity are overthrown when these areas of sacred doctrine are neglected, over-
shadowed or compromised. In reaction to this, actual reformation needed to take place, and even in this present day still
must take place. It would do the church well to have 1) theologians who rightly know the Word in such a way as to stand
upon it in the face of any other unorthodox views that attempt
to corrupt the true doctrines of the faith, 2) pastors who are
well equipped to train and teach these doctrines to the church,
and 3) laymen who are willing to receive such teaching in the
faced of popular Christianity. If the areas of higher education
were theologically sound, and that education transferred both
theologically and practically to pastors who desire to teach the
people of God the Word of God, and the people of God desired
to hold to such sound doctrine and practical teaching, the
church would be a far different place than it is today as a whole.
If Calvin were alive today, he would have to write the same tract
again, but with a more pressing angle since the church so easily
is swayed by every wind of doctrine, and every popular level of
Evangelicalism.

The subtitle of Calvin's polemic is, *Seriously To Undertake
The Task Of Restoring The Church*, and it is dedicated, "In The
Name Of All Who Wish Christ To Reign." Calvin desired to repair the improper worship of God, and bring the church back to
a pure worship that honors Christ. Calvin was not willing to
simply "undertake" reformation, but "seriously to undertake
the task" of restoring the biblical Gospel to the worship and life
of the Church. The Scriptural rule of worship should be fol-

lowed as accurately as it is stated and exemplified in the Word of God. This rule, or principle, distinguishes between pure worship that is of universal application by God's command, and human folly that changes worship into "will-worship," or the worship of "the self" instead of God. "We should," as Calvin says, "strictly enjoin what he wishes us to do," as well as "at once" reject every human invention that does not line up with the Word of God. Calvin presses the immediate need for reformation in worship that does not strictly adhere to the commandment of the Word. But he did not stop there. In adhering to the regulative principles found in the Word of God, these principles not only regulate the worship of the church, but also extend or are annexed to "all the actions of our lives." This meant that the church was only one sphere in which reform should take place. True biblical Reformation will affect every area of the Christian life. It will affect the Church, the Home, Society, places of employment, in a word – everywhere. The practical outworking of following the Regulative Principle is its extensions in a right ordering of life in general after the Word of God. But this cannot happen without having a right heart for Reformation.

Those who have a heart after true biblical Reformation will ultimately see a change in the manner that the Christian religion brings them *coram deo*, before the face of God. Such a Reformation, through the true Gospel of Jesus Christ and justification by faith alone, will unite Christians to God in a more intimate manner than what pop Christianity can offer on some emotional high. Such pop Christianity is not true biblical Christianity. Today, smorgasbord niceties are packaged within the term "Evangelicalism." But current Evangelicalism is not the same as it was during the time of the Reformation, or of any time of "reformation" through the history of the biblical narratives of God's people. During the Reformation, the term "Evangelical" was used to describe the reformers who believed in "gospelling" or heralding the good news of justification by faith alone. In contrast to the Roman Catholic Church of the day, Protestants were known as these "Evangelicals." Those in league with Wittenberg and the Swiss cantons toward Reformation were frequently referred to as Evangelical by the Roman Church. Reformation doctrine, then, historically, was associated with the term "reformed". And in those days "reformed" meant something very specific. However, today, this is not the case. Evangelicalism does not have a heart for reformation any longer. They are more interested in theology dispensed by "Christian cartoons" or popular TV and radio preachers. In general the term "Evangelical" has developed into a more inclusivistic attitude toward liberalism, and is ecumenical in its worldwide efforts towards "ecclesiastical unity". As a result of a broad churchism this non-theological view is akin to simply pleasing the masses.

The Evangelical sector is made up of pastors, theologians and teachers who are best described as "theologically flexible." This is an oversimplification for many of them. This ecumenical and theological flexibility is a key factor (and problem) among contemporary Evangelicals. They are often noncompulsory and convicting in their preaching, and desire to keep "peace" in their churches for the sake of ecumenicalism. The problem that is faced is their flagrant inability to draw solid nonnegotiable doctrinal lines in the sand. And solid nonnegotiable doctrinal lines are what sparked every reformation from those accounted in the biblical narratives, to those that surrounded the Reformation of the 16th century, to the post-Reformation dogmatics that emerged as a result of fine tuning theology accomplish by English Puritanism during the 17th century, and the Great Awakenings later in the histories of England and America. In other words, to have reformation, one needs sound doctrine. But it is unfortunate that the church must look *back* in history to find those great old-aged redwood theologians. Why is it that they cannot look in their own churches?

When Christian book catalogues come to this writer's door, it is always interesting to find out what current Evangelicals think are the "best" books, or what books are "top sellers." In the latest catalogue to come by (a January / March Winter Catalogue), it housed 64 pages, of which only two had room for any books that were worthwhile, or even close to begin "biblically accurate." When opening up the catalogue, it begins with their "top sellers." Now in perusing these top sellers, what is listed? Rick Warren's "Purpose Driven Life," and directly beneath that is his "Purpose Driven Church." Under that is found Max Lucado's "Come Thirsty", and just to the right is found "Your Best Life Now" by Joel Osteen. Just to the right of that, in a final column, is Joyce Meyers's two latest books, "Approval Addiction: Overcoming Your Need to Please Everyone," and "Battlefield of the Mind" – updated Edition (as if another is needed). Yes, Benny Hinn is there too with some of his works, and charismaniacs adorn the rest of this section. With "top sellers" like these books written by theological morons and false teachers, one does not have to wonder too long why the American church is dying! What the church needs to do is stop worrying about the dollar and how much money one can make by selling theological drivel, and begin caring about what pleases God. Certainly, with nonsense like these books, and their watered down version of the Gospel (and certainly contrary versions of the Gospel), hitting the Christian marketplace, and making them top sellers, the church is 1) ignorant of the truth, and 2) in desperate need of a thorough reformation that is Christ-glorifying.

Reformation is always something that is accomplished *thoroughly* as well. Again, be reminded, historically speaking, being *reformed* meant something *specific*. It should be agreed that being "Reformed" or going about "Reformation" meant something to Ulrich Zwingli, William Tyndale, Martin Luther, John Calvin and other reformers. History, though, gives way to how it is accomplished practically. It is not something that men are allowed to take in "part" in the name of "reforming" or simply to be associated with that which is "reformed". Men ought not say they are all for "true biblical reformation" if they could not, in good conscience, claim the entirety of the Reformed faith if they simply believed one tenth of what the Reformation taught, or what the Bible teaches about true biblical Reformation. Also, they could not, in good conscience call themselves Reformed or claim the Reformed faith if they simply believed nine tenths of what the Reformation taught, and rejected the other one tenth completely. They must, of necessity, embrace Reformation doctrine to claim the Reformed banner. In like manner they cannot believe four points of the five points of Calvinism and call themselves a Calvinist. Those who believe the doctrines of grace know this little ploy used too well by confused Arminians who say such things. But the orthodox know such doctrinal deviation is wrong, or at the very least, they know that such people are extremely confused. It is much the same with the doctrines of the Reformation, and what the bible teaches about true biblical reformation. One cannot reject Reformed worship, those foundational guidelines within the orthodox realm of Reformed doctrine, and say they are Reformed. They cannot discard church discipline and say they are Reformed. They cannot reject key aspects of Covenant Theology and call themselves Reformed. They cannot misuse the sacraments, or deny them, and call themselves Reformed. Holding to certain biblical ideologies determines whether one is Reformed or not. In all of this, the reader must ask themselves, "Do I really have a heart for true biblical reformation?" It is the nature and purpose of this work to take that question and remove it from its normally posed historical aspect, and place it in the realm of what the Bible practically says about "reforming" and what true biblical reformation can do for the church if it welcomes it with open arms.

Leviticus 26:23-24, "And if by these things you are not *reformed* by Me, but walk contrary to Me, then I also will walk contrary to you, and I will punish you yet seven times for your sins."

Hebrews 9:9-10, "It was symbolic for the present time in which both gifts and sacrifices are offered which cannot make him who performed the service perfect in regard to the conscience concerned only with foods and drinks, various washings, and fleshly ordinances imposed until the time of *reformation*."

For His glory,
Dr. C. Matthew McMahon
May 4, 2007
Coconut Creek, FL

"What the Reformation really means is simply *Reformation*: that is, the decay and removal of a previous system of unreal and false religion to make room for that which is real and true."

- William Wileman, History of the Reformation

❧ 1 ❧

What is Reformation?

Second Kings 22:1 - 23:25, "Josiah *was* eight years old when he became king, and he reigned thirty-one years in Jerusalem. His mother's name *was* Jedidah the daughter of Adaiah of Bozkath. ² And he did *what was* right in the sight of the LORD, and walked in all the ways of his father David; he did not turn aside to the right hand or to the left. ³ Now it came to pass, in the eighteenth year of King Josiah, *that* the king sent Shaphan the scribe, the son of Azaliah, the son of Meshullam, to the house of the LORD, saying: ⁴ "Go up to Hilkiah the high priest, that he may count the money which has been brought into the house of the LORD, which the doorkeepers have gathered from the people. ⁵ "And let them deliver it into the hand of those doing the work, who are the overseers in the house of the LORD; let them give it to those who *are* in the house of the LORD doing the work, to repair the damages of the house -- ⁶ "to carpenters and builders and masons -- and to buy timber and hewn stone to repair the house. ⁷ "However there need be no accounting made with them of the money delivered into their hand, because they deal faithfully." ⁸ Then Hilkiah the high priest said to Shaphan the scribe, "I have found the Book of the Law in the house of the LORD." And Hilkiah gave the book to

Shaphan, and he read it. 9 So Shaphan the scribe went to the king, bringing the king word, saying, "Your servants have gathered the money that was found in the house, and have delivered it into the hand of those who do the work, who oversee the house of the LORD." 10 Then Shaphan the scribe showed the king, saying, "Hilkiah the priest has given me a book." And Shaphan read it before the king. 11 Now it happened, when the king heard the words of the Book of the Law, that he tore his clothes. 12 Then the king commanded Hilkiah the priest, Ahikam the son of Shaphan, Achbor the son of Michaiah, Shaphan the scribe, and Asaiah a servant of the king, saying, 13 "Go, inquire of the LORD for me, for the people and for all Judah, concerning the words of this book that has been found; for great *is* the wrath of the LORD that is aroused against us, because our fathers have not obeyed the words of this book, to do according to all that is written concerning us." 14 So Hilkiah the priest, Ahikam, Achbor, Shaphan, and Asaiah went to Huldah the prophetess, the wife of Shallum the son of Tikvah, the son of Harhas, keeper of the wardrobe. (She dwelt in Jerusalem in the Second Quarter.) And they spoke with her. 15 Then she said to them, "Thus says the LORD God of Israel, 'Tell the man who sent you to Me, 16 "Thus says the LORD: 'Behold, I will bring calamity on this place and on its inhabitants -- all the words of the book which the king of Judah has read -- 17 'because they have forsaken Me and burned incense to other gods, that they might provoke Me to anger with all the works of their hands. Therefore My wrath shall be aroused against this place and shall not be quenched.' 18 "But as for the king of Judah, who sent you to inquire of the LORD, in this manner you shall speak to him, 'Thus says the LORD God of Israel: "*Concerning* the words which you have heard -- 19 "because your heart was tender, and you humbled yourself before the LORD when you heard what I spoke against this place and against its inhabitants, that they would become a desolation and a curse, and you tore your clothes and wept before Me, I also have heard *you,*" says the LORD. ²⁰ "Surely, therefore, I will gather you to your fathers, and you shall be gathered to your grave in peace; and your eyes shall not see all the calamity which I will bring on this place." So they brought back word to the king."

23:1 Now the king sent them to gather all the elders of Judah and Jerusalem to him. ² The king went up to the house of the LORD with all the men of Judah, and with him all the inhabitants of Jerusalem -- the priests and the prophets and all the people, both small and great. And he read in their hearing all the words of the Book of the Covenant which had been found in the house of the LORD. ³ Then the king stood by a pillar and made a covenant before the LORD, to follow the LORD and to keep His commandments and His testimonies and His statutes, with all *his* heart and all *his* soul, to perform the words of this covenant that were written in this book. And all the people took a stand for the covenant. ⁴ And the king commanded Hilkiah the high priest, the priests of the second order, and the doorkeepers, to bring out of the temple of the LORD all the articles that were made for Baal, for Asherah, and for all the host of heaven; and he burned them outside Jerusalem in the fields of Kidron, and carried their ashes to Bethel. ⁵ Then he removed the idolatrous priests whom the kings of Judah had ordained to burn incense on the high places in the cities of Judah and in the places all around Jerusalem, and those who burned incense to Baal, to the sun, to the moon, to the constellations, and to all the host of heaven. ⁶ And he brought out the wooden image from the house of the LORD, to the Brook Kidron outside Jerusalem, burned it at the Brook Kidron and ground *it* to ashes, and threw its ashes on the graves of the common people. ⁷ Then he tore down the *ritual* booths of the perverted persons that *were* in the house of the LORD, where the women wove hangings for the wooden image. ⁸ And he brought all the priests from the cities of Judah, and defiled the high places where the priests had burned incense, from Geba to Beersheba; also he broke down the high places at the gates which *were* at the entrance of the Gate of Joshua the governor of the city, which *were* to the left of the city gate. ⁹ Nevertheless the priests of the high places did not come up to the altar of the LORD in Jerusalem, but they ate unleavened bread among their brethren. ¹⁰ And he defiled Topheth, which *is* in the Valley of the Son of Hinnom, that no man might make his son or his daughter pass through the fire to Molech. ¹¹ Then he removed the horses that the kings of Judah had dedicated to the sun, at the entrance to the house of the LORD, by the chamber of Nathan-Melech, the officer who *was* in the court; and he burned the chariots of the sun with fire. ¹² The altars that *were* on the roof, the upper chamber of Ahaz, which the kings of Judah had made, and the altars which Manasseh had made in the two courts of the house of the LORD, the king broke down and pulverized there, and threw their dust into the Brook Kidron. ¹³ Then the king defiled the high places that *were* east of Jerusalem, which *were* on the south of the Mount of Corruption, which Solomon king of Israel had built for Ashtoreth the abomination of the Sidonians, for Chemosh the abomination of the Moabites, and for Milcom the abomination of the people of Ammon. ¹⁴ And he broke in pieces the *sacred* pillars and cut down the wooden images, and filled their places with the bones of men. ¹⁵ Moreover the altar that *was* at Bethel, *and* the high place which Jeroboam the son of Nebat, who made Israel sin, had made, both that altar and the high place he broke down; and he burned the high place *and* crushed *it* to powder, and burned the wooden image. ¹⁶ As Josiah turned, he saw the tombs that *were* there on the mountain. And he sent and took the bones out of the tombs and burned *them* on the altar, and defiled it according to the word of the

LORD which the man of God proclaimed, who proclaimed these words. ¹⁷ Then he said, "What gravestone *is* this that I see?" So the men of the city told him, "*It is* the tomb of the man of God who came from Judah and proclaimed these things which you have done against the altar of Bethel." ¹⁸ And he said, "Let him alone; let no one move his bones." So they let his bones alone, with the bones of the prophet who came from Samaria. ¹⁹ Now Josiah also took away all the shrines of the high places that *were* in the cities of Samaria, which the kings of Israel had made to provoke the LORD to anger; and he did to them according to all the deeds he had done in Bethel. ²⁰ He executed all the priests of the high places who *were* there, on the altars, and burned men's bones on them; and he returned to Jerusalem. ²¹ Then the king commanded all the people, saying, "Keep the Passover to the LORD your God, as *it is* written in this Book of the Covenant." ²² Such a Passover surely had never been held since the days of the judges who judged Israel, nor in all the days of the kings of Israel and the kings of Judah. ²³ But in the eighteenth year of King Josiah this Passover was held before the LORD in Jerusalem. ²⁴ Moreover Josiah put away those who consulted mediums and spiritists, the household gods and idols, all the abominations that were seen in the land of Judah and in Jerusalem, that he might perform the words of the law which were written in the book that Hilkiah the priest found in the house of the LORD. ²⁵ Now before him there was no king like him, who turned to the LORD with all his heart, with all his soul, and with all his might, according to all the Law of Moses; nor after him did *any* arise like him."

Considering the Text

Regularly, taking into account such a long text would be a mistake. Long passages often lose their flavor and ideas are often lost when they are not expositorily demonstrated over long pages of careful exegesis. However, in this instance, it is far better to deal with a longer text since the narrative itself explains so much, and most of what is happening in these two chapters is hard to miss.

In briefly considering the text at hand, the narrative moves from Josiah's ascension to the throne, to a revival among the kingdom due to the discovery of the Book of the Law. In 22:1-2 Josiah becomes King and these verses open the reign of Josiah with the conventional introductory formula for the reign of a king from Judah. Previously, Manasseh and Amon had been kings over Judah. It is Josiah's unfortunate timing that allows him to come into a situation already gone badly. Manasseh reigned the longest (fifty-five years), and Amon one of the shortest (two years)[1]. Both of these kings were wicked in the eyes of the Lord, and subjected the people to false gods, idols, and all kinds of abominations. The Scriptures say of him, "Manasseh seduced them to do more evil than the nations whom the LORD had destroyed before the children of Israel" (2 Kings 21:9). God was so displeased and angry with the sins of Manasseh and the people's willingness to be seduced by his wickedness, that the Lord said, "Behold, I am bringing such calamity upon Jerusalem and Judah, that whoever hears of it, both his ears will tingle" (2 Kings 21:12). Literally the Hebrew "tingle" means "to quiver with fear." The people seeing the calamity that God would bring will be "astonished" at it. This was the kingdom that Amon continued, and Josiah inherited.

In 22:3–7 we have the author of Kings recounting the redistribution of the temple collection to facilitate the repairs to the temple. The author quickly moves to the most outstanding example of Josiah's godly fidelity: his repair of the temple in his

---

[1] It seems Shallum reigned the shortest, one month, due to his assassination (2 Kings 15:13). But in an overall survey of the kings, two years, though applied to a few of them, were short reigns.

eighteenth year which would be around 622 B.C. It should be noted, however, that 2 Chronicles 34:3 says that at age sixteen Josiah was already demonstrating his piety to the God of David. The text reads, "For in the eighth year of his reign, while he was yet young, he began to seek after the God of David his father: and in the twelfth year he began to purge Judah and Jerusalem from the high places, and the groves, and the carved images, and the molten images." The text also says, "of David his father." The author uses here a spiritual example – as David was a man after God's own heart, so Josiah is a man after God's own heart as well. Josiah is like his father David, not his father Amon, or his grandfather Manasseh. In this, it is easy to see the regenerating work of the Spirit of God already moving upon this king who has a spirit different than his wicked father and grandfather. With such a man God can do much. This is why Josiah, and not Amon or Manasseh, is given the providential blessing of finding the Book of the Law. Those with wicked hearts burn God's word and reject it (cf. the burning of the Word by Jehoiakim in Jeremiah 36:26-27). Those with hearts after God's heart love His word and receive it. As David said in Psalm 119:105, "Your word is a lamp to my feet and a light to my path."

In 2 Kings 22:8–11 there is Josiah's reaction to the finding of the law-book. Josiah's men were to facilitate the rebuilding and refurbishing of the temple which had lain in ruins. The spiritual decay of the people reflected in their want of conformity to upholding the temple as God prescribed. It fell into disarray. And Josiah's outstanding piety would be reflected in restoring the place of central worship to the people. But something occurs here that is unexpected. Hilkiah, while tallying the building materials the laborers would need to complete restoration, finds the Book of the Law. Was this the Pentateuch? According to the description of the author of Kings, it certainly was the Law of Moses. The author's commentary on 2 Kings 23:24-25 helps greatly, "Moreover Josiah put away those who consulted mediums and spiritists, the household gods and idols, all the abominations that were seen in the land of Judah and in Jerusalem, that he might perform the words of the law which were written in the book that Hilkiah the priest found in the house of the LORD. Now before him there was no king like him, who turned to the LORD with all his heart, with all his soul, and with all his might, according to all the Law of Moses; nor after him did any arise like him." The "Law of Moses" is the Book of Moses. It is the penned revelation of Genesis-Deuteronomy inscribed by Moses. It holds in it the revelation of creation, the lives of the patriarchs, the preservation of the family line, to the establishment of the Law of God, and the covenantal bounds that the people of God would have through this Law with God. Hilkiah gives the book to Shaphan after identifying it as the Law of Moses, and Shaphan reads it. He in turn immediately brings it to the King. Shaphan interjects, as a faithful servant, a report of what has transpired with facilitating the money needed for the laborers of the temple. That is good news to the king – but there is better news to come.

After the initial report of the monies collected and delivered, Shaphan "shows" the King the Book of the Law that Hilkiah the priest found in the temple. What would Josiah's reaction to this book be? Shaphan reads Josiah the book. No doubt this took some time to read all the Law. Would the king sit through a reading of the law? Would he storm out? Would he burn it? What would the King's reaction be to their current relationship to the Word of Yahweh? The people have wallowed in wickedness for so long, and Josiah had done some good among the people, and was well on the way to restoring the temple. But was this even close to being enough? Josiah's reaction to the Law is astounding. He "tears his clothes". The tearing of the clothes symbolized the tearing away of wicked-ness and sin. It was a lamenting of great anguish which placed men bare before God, with no "covering" laid open before His omniscient gaze. It was symbolic, but it symbolized much for the Jewish mind. He was sorely lamenting the state of his kinsmen, and his own sin, before the face of God. Keep in mind this is a twenty-six year old "young man". Most twenty-six year olds today are still wet behind the ears and have barely come to a sound point of maturity. They are out partying. In contrast, Josiah enters into an act of deep contrition and lamenting for the sins of Judah before God.

What is the reaction to hearing God's Word? There was no question in his mind as to what the Book of the Law said. It seems Christians often have a hard time "discerning the will of the Lord" when reading the Scriptures, and coming away with a less than clear attainment of what God generally desires His people to believe. It is much easier to have an emotional ex-perience with God than it is to study hard and come away with a sound understanding of a passage of Scripture. But Josiah's experience was *informed* by the Word of God. The Scriptures are not convoluted and difficult so as to restrict any immediate action when such things are so plain. Josiah knew exactly what the Scriptures said, and how he and the people had failed to keep God's Law. This is akin to the exact opposite reaction un-der Jeremiah's ministry when Jehoiakim burns the scroll, the Word of God. Jehoiakim too understands the message of the Word of God, but in return he *hates* it. Josiah understands its message and is repentant for their sin.

As a result of sin, Josiah must inquire as to what God will do to them. Josiah knows that God will do "something" for their sin. So he inquires of a prophetess to gain information on God's next move. He then sends a convoy to Huldah the prophetess. Huldah gives them a terrifying message. 2 Kings

22:12-20 spells out the impending doom for the people. God
will not relent of the wickedness of Judah. God threatens great
destruction on the people for their sin. But Josiah is not de-
spondent. Even though judgment is coming, and the people
will be judged, the right response to the Book of the Law is to
rectify what is wrong. The threatenings press Josiah to act even
though God will not allow Josiah to see the calamity coming. In
22:18-20 it is explicit that calamity will still ensue, regardless of
the reforms that Josiah will make, but it would be a greater sin
to have the light of the Word and not make those reforms for
the glory of God. Even though Josiah will set up a hearty reform, God's judgment will not be dissuaded. But this makes
little difference to the righteous. Those who are righteous desire to see righteous rule across the land and will do everything
needed to make that their aim and goal. So Josiah makes a covenant with the people.

2 Kings 23:1-3 demonstrates the inauguration of a covenant
with *all* the people, not simply between Josiah and God. Josiah
calls all of the people to come together at a specific point at the
temple. He stands by "the column" of the temple, signifying his
authority, surrounding the simile of *foundational* authority. At
this foundational point of the temple, at this foundational time
in the history of Judah, Josiah renews the Covenant which was
previously made at Sinai. It is "covenant renewal" due to their
lack of covenant obedience. A "covenant" is *a pact or agreement made between two parties.* This is the idea and connotation of "covenant" all through the Old Testament and New Testament. As the *Westminster Confession of Faith* states, a covenant holds in it the basic concepts of "life promised upon the
condition of perfect and personal obedience."[2] Josiah presses
the people to willingly take a renewed stance in the Law by upholding it bound by covenant.

---

[2] *The Westminster Confession of Faith*, 7:2: Of God's Covenant with Man.

Not only did Josiah enact a covenant with the people, but the text says, "...the people took a stand" in it. Here it means to "be in a standing attitude" or even has connotations of becoming a *slave* to it.

They were utterly bound by covenant to uphold the Word of God. Such a covenant held in it blessings if they kept it, and curses if they broke it. God would bless them abundantly if they upheld the words of the Law, but would curse them if they broke their solemn vow against Him. Making a covenant to uphold God's Word is a covenant made with God Himself, for His Word and His being are essentially the same. God Himself is the Living Word (cf. John 1:1ff). In this oath or vow to uphold the Law, Josiah is essentially enacting a *covenanted reformation*. The people are "covenanting" together to perform what is necessary for reformation to occur. Josiah, the elders, the priests and all the people swear to uphold this covenant with God even though Josiah knows he will not dissuade God's righteous judgment on Judah after his own death. This, in and of itself, is a rather amazing act on his part, and a testimony to all who come after him. Though impending judgment will not be reverted, Josiah, in essence, presses the people to be more responsible for their sin by fixing what they can in the time they have.

The outward act of Josiah's *Covenanted Reformation* begins in 2 Kings 23:4–20. Here there is an account of the purging of the cult in Jerusalem and Judah of Canaanite practices. First, Josiah has them bring out of the temple all the articles of other gods intruding on God's worship. Such "mixing" of religion (or what is called Religious Syncretism) cannot be tolerated. It must be utterly destroyed. Josiah has these articles burned. Next, he removed the idolatrous priests and recalls the Levitical priests from their duties at various high places. Even places previously missed by Hezekiah's short reform (cf. 2 Chronicles

29:1ff) were now thoroughly destroyed. Josiah was not simply content with destroying the high places and burning the Asherah poles. He exhumed the human bones from the graves situated on the mountain and burned them on the altar, thus defiling it forever. He burned the wooden images and threw them on the common graves defiling the images and showing their commonality or anti-sacredness. This burning and grinding to dust is a gesture of absolute destruction, of turning something from its form into chaos. Such gestures as this were not to defile the graves (Josiah would never desire to defile the graves of his people); it is contact with *dead bodies* which defiles. Rather, the Asherah, now ground to dust, was placed where it belonged in the outlook of the reformer—with the dead. Josiah defiled the pagan altars, removed the priests, pulverized the altars and scattered their dust.

Josiah did not stop with the removal of the inanimate objects, but he also executed all the priests of the high places, and burned their bones as well. He rid the country of spiritists and mediums, household gods, and "all abominations..." seen in the land according to the Word of God, the Book of the Law. Could these false priests be reformed? Should Josiah have tried reasoning with them? Is God more interested in evangelizing them than killing them? No. They were to be utterly destroyed as a result of rejecting the Word of the God and teaching others to do so.[3] Amos 2:4 depicts the judgment against them for this, "For three transgressions of Judah, and for four, I will not turn away its punishment, because they have despised the law of the LORD, and have not kept His commandments. Their lies lead

---

[3] In comparison to modern evangelicals, God seems to have a strange manner about His type of evangelism. Modern Evangelicals would have set up a 12-step program to bring the idolatrous priests back to their senses, and then reinstated them after a time. God, though, through Josiah, has much different plans. Remember, God commended Josiah for his actions as a testimony in the Scriptures for his righteous judgments and true reformation.

them astray, lies which their fathers followed." Such an admonition in the Book of the Law is echoed by the Savior in Matthew 18:6, "But whoever causes one of these little ones who believe in Me to sin, it would be better for him if a millstone were hung around his neck, and he were drowned in the depth of the sea." Josiah completed a thorough reform and no stone was left unturned. Rather, the stones were heaped upon those false teachers who lead the people astray with lying words.

After the reform took place, and the high places and idols destroyed, Josiah enacts a celebration. 2 Kings 23:21–23 provides a brief reference to the inauguration of a Passover celebration in Jerusalem at the king's initiative. He reestablished right worship, and the center of worship was at Jerusalem according to the book of the Law. He instituted, again, *right* worship. Previously, they were *not* engaging in right worship, but *wrong* worship, which means *there is a difference* between one and the other. If everything is okay, and various styles and tastes are okay in the life of the church and its worship, then the Book of the Law would not have mattered to Josiah. In today's church culture, every form of man's vain imaginations are tossed into the life and worship of the church, but people fail to see the danger of it all. It is not okay to simply change worship, or God's will in worship, and think God accepts that worship because it "gets results." Rather, as Josiah saw it, so today the church *should* see it as abominable. Worship never changes toward a God who is immutably set and regulates such worship by His Word. God's Word *never* changes, nor should our worship of Him in the manner that He alone prescribes. To change or add to the worship God has set down is to deem our fallible human wisdom more righteous than God's commands.

Right worship does not surround what men can do or think they should do, but what God desires and wants for His church. Josiah's first inauguration of positive (or right) worship was the institution of sacramental blood, and atonement, found in the Passover. Substitutionary sacrificial atonement was his first act of worship with the people of God. It was not parades and puppet shows. It was a reinstituting what they had previously forgotten and left out.

After this celebration, Josiah is commended. 2 Kings 23:24–25 demonstrates his continued reforms as well as an editorial comment on the piety of the king. "Now before him there was no king like him, who turned to the LORD with all his heart, with all his soul, and with all his might, according to all the Law of Moses; nor after him did any arise like him." The Hebrew concept behind "turned to the Lord with all his heart" means "to turn back, return to God, and repent." Josiah shines as an outstanding example, the best example, of destroying that which is not pleasing to God, instituting what is pleasing to God, and the manner in which one is to do it.

What 2 Kings 22-23 Can Teach Us About Being Reformed and Reforming

There are three important propositions that can be drawn from this narrative that continually affect the church of God in any age. First, True Biblical Reformation is only accomplished through the Word of God. Second, True Biblical Reformation is always joined to a solemn resolve to continue to follow God's Word. Third, True Biblical Reformation is always a thorough reform. Without adhering to these three maxims, reformation in the church will *never* take place.

First, *True Biblical Reformation is only accomplished through the Word of God.* This should be rather simple to accept. If one speaks of "true biblical reformation" then it is imposed by the Bible and is true according to the Word of God. Such a reformation or "reforming" of past improper ways and actions can only come to light in view of God's Word and His desires for reformation. The things that interest a theologically disinterested contemporary American church are *not* right worship, and are *not* conforming to God's law. Instead, the contemporary American church, even the modern 21st century church through the world, is profoundly affected by a postmodern distinctive of existentialism. There is too much "Jesus loves "this" (whatever "this" may be) and I know it because my *heart* tells me so." It is the plague of corporate relativism which *deunificates* the church. "I know its right worship because it feels so good." "I know it is a good church because the pastor is friendly." "I know it is God honoring because so many other people feel the same way I do." Statements like these are found in most churches and are the affects of the post-modern mind that is giving itself over and over to the relativism empowered by secularism. It is the religious syncretism that permeated the church in Josiah's day all over *again*.

One may ask, "What is Biblical Reformation by the Word?" To remedy the relativism of the contemporary church, this is an important question to answer. The word "reformation" should be defined properly, if reforming is the goal of the church in glorifying God. Without understanding what it means to "reform" the church will never be able to please God in *reforming*. "Reformation" or "being reformed" means "to be chastened, admonished or corrected by the Bible, and to conform to that chastening, that correction or that admonition." That is a good definition of "reformed" for the purposes of this text. If Josiah did nothing after hearing the Word of God, no reformation would have taken place. It is imperative, then, that no matter how much true biblical "reformation" may change or hurt personal feelings or individual theological views, it should be noted that such personal views do not trump the Word of God. Personal views, personal interests, or relativism of any kind must be utterly destroyed by the Word of God and right views and right theology must be set in place over and against such things. It does not matter what Mrs. Smith thinks about worship, or what Mr. Jones does or does not like. What matters is what God commands and instructs His people to conform to that makes the difference. Otherwise, churches that disregard God's intention for His people in worship are being idolaters. Thus, churches would do well in recounting God's Word and instituting only what God has commanded in worship, rather than trying to appease congregations with what will draw in crowds.

Think about what Josiah initially *had*. He was in the center of religious worship in Jerusalem. He had the temple (a church building). He had a big church building – one of a kind by all estimations – even more grand than the religious multiplex of the Willowcreek church with its restaurants and snack bars, or the Crystal Cathedral with its towering glimmers and columns of glass. Josiah even had a right heart that desired to repair the temple. He appealed to the people for a collection, and the people responded; so there was a measure of religiosity in the country. In such things, people oftentimes feel guilty or want simply to be included in the "giving." But it was coupled with religious syncretism, the mixing of pagan rites, and elements of right worship. Yet remember, to mix worship in this way is to *destroy* it – and religion in general was so utterly devastated by Manasseh and Amon that Josiah was repairing the temple brought to disarray from *neglect*. Overall, though, they were *religious people*. People can be religious and never see a hint of true biblical reformation back to the Word of God. People all over the world are religious, but that does not mean God is pleased, nor does it mean He accepts them or their practices. God certainly does accept the worship of those who are religious. But such religious people are those that religiously conform to what God desires for them in worship according to the Scriptures.

People in America are so used to getting what they want, they forget and are numbed to what God commands of them, or simply, they have never learned it. Josiah had elders, priests, and even a high priest. These were religious instructors. Many churches have religious instructors who can teach you how you can have purpose in forty days or how you can pray a magic prayer and increase your borders with amazing personal prosperity. Some religious teachers have even taught that since God has golden garbage cans, then you too should have golden garbage cans and prosper as much as God does. This, however, is not what God intends for true biblical reformation. True biblical reformation is only going to be accomplished through the Word of God. There are no shortcuts to it. Pithy quotes, magic prayers, contemporary plans of corporate success for the church do not matter to God. They are simply a distraction formulated by a smart devil to neutralize the power of God in the church. It does not matter how popular or charismatic a preacher may be in the 21st century, and how many people he can persuade to visit his church. Big churches are often a sign of spiritual decay, not of religious blessing. How many popular preachers are there across the United States alone and how degraded has the country become without so much as even a "reformed" ripple? And people think they are being blessed by such a ministry? In Josiah's day they thought that too. Such churches that replace true biblical reformation with religious pragmatism should simply post "Manasseh was here" across the doorposts, or "Ichabod – the glory had departed." Without the Word of God such charisma, such flamboyant preaching, will never be pleasing or acceptable to sovereign Lord who dispenses grace through *truth* to His people.

Josiah also had religious objects: altars, sacrificial stones, wooden images, incense and the like. Fancy Pews, crystal pulpits, Christian bumper stickers, gold crosses hanging from the neck, and WWJD bracelets are rubbish without the Word of God. They have a form of godliness but deny its power. They are just "gadgets for God."

Josiah had lots of things in his *face*, but nothing in his *ear* to travel into his mind and ignite his heart. Josiah did not have the Word of God initially. But anyone today can walk into a grocery store and pick up a $5 copy of the Bible, and churches all over the world continually neglect it to satisfy their own tastes, their own corporate style of leadership, their own method of worship, and they are sacrificing people on the altars of ignorance at the expense of the Word of God. Such misinformed preachers, theologians and pastors function like pied pipers who whistle a tune that itching ears want to hear and as a result droves of ignorant people follow them like rats into the river. It is no wonder that God says "My people are destroyed from a lack of knowledge" (Hosea 4:6).

What changed Josiah? When he had heard the Word of the Lord, he was struck down in lamentation and bitter weeping, he tore his clothes. What Christian, pastor, theologian, etc., have you ever seen tear his clothes? (Or the equivalent?)

The catalyst for Reformation is always the Word of God. It was Martin Luther's wrestling with the righteousness of God in the Word of God that sparked the massive overhaul in the Reformation of the Church. It was his dedication to the Word of God that made his name great. It was not a new style of salvation and worship that Luther came up with, but getting *back to the old style*. It was recovering that which was lost. 2 Kings 23:25 uses such an excellent term four times to this end - "the whole of it" or the word "all" – "all the Law of Moses". The people swore before God at the temple to be careful to do all that is written in the law. They would uphold all of it. Like Luther much later in the history of the church, Josiah and the people held unswervingly to the Word of God, and all of the

Word of God (not parts of it). In doing so, they found that true biblical reformation would only be accomplished by following God's Word, and not their own twisted dictates or desires.

Secondly, *True biblical Reformation is always joined to a solemn resolve to continue to follow God's Word.* Josiah did not simply make a few adjustments, but performed, by *oath*, a solemn league with the people of Judah to return to serving God acceptably and with godly fear. The text reads in 2 Kings 23:3, "Then the king stood by a pillar and made a *covenant* before the LORD, to follow the LORD and to keep *His* commandments and *His* testimonies and *His* statutes, with all his heart and all his soul, to perform the words of this covenant that were written in this book. And all the people took a stand for the *covenant*." Is there anything wrong with following the command of God here? Could the people have wavered in the intent of the King? No, they could not have wavered and they could not reject this oath. They could not say "I do not feel right making an oath." It would be akin to saying "I do not believe the Word of God and I do not want to accomplish it or follow it." Josiah would have had such a person stoned as he did the false priests who taught people to believe a lie. So a lawful oath, being imposed by lawful authority, in such matters, *ought to be taken.*

In historic England, there was a problem surrounding being unified in religion and worship. A clear call for an assembly of divines, whose task would be to advise the government on the reformation of the Church, was summoned through the speeches of the members of the Long Parliament and in sermons of preachers who addressed the members at Westminster – these cries were heard from 1641-1642. There was need for a national synod to advise Parliament on what form the National Church and Religion should now take. After five successive failures a bill finally passed through both Houses in June, 1643, which called the Westminster Assembly of Divines into being. Parliament took the task of calling together a committee in which could revise the Thirty-nine Articles of Religion for the times. A committee was set down for this purpose, but later it was thought that a convocation of divines should come together for an entire revamping of the religious system of government now being imposed on the entire island. It was here that the Westminster Assembly was called together. King Charles never agreed to the calling of a synod of divines even though Parliament prepared and agreed to several bills for this purpose. An ordinance was given to call together these divines. The ordinance shows that the principal concern of Parliament at this stage was the reformation of the government of the Church and the "vindicating and clearing of the doctrine of the Church of England from all false calumnies and aspersions." One hundred and twenty ministers and thirty laymen were invited to attend. The Assembly first met on July 1st, 1643, in Westminster Abbey. But the Assembly could not continue in good conscience without first coming together in a *solemn* purpose for the good of religion under a unified vow. This vow was called, "The Solemn League and Covenant." After it had a commission to be put to paper, it was drafted, accepted unanimously, and then read before the Assembly. The Westminster Assembly covenanted together first before beginning any theological debates because purpose of mind is first needful before true biblical reformation will ever take place. The reason churches today will not go back to adhering to the *Solemn League and Covenant* is because it is a straight jacket to them. Vows are straight jackets. It is, to them, God in a box. Rather, the contemporary church wants to open their doctrinal doors so wide that anything is allowed to come flowing in that they believe the "Spirit desires". But they forget, or they are simply ignorant, that the Spirit has already written down what He desires by way of obedience for the church in the Word of God. Lawful oaths or vows, then, are a crucial aspect to seeing fruit in true biblical reformation.

The Westminster Confession of Faith makes plain, "A lawful oath is a part of religious worship, wherein, upon just occasion, the person swearing solemnly calls God to witness what he asserts, or promises, and to judge him according to the truth or falsehood of what he swears."[4] This is substantiated by the same Law that Josiah read in Deuteronomy 10:20, "You shall fear the LORD your God; you shall serve Him, and to Him you shall hold fast, and take oaths in His name." This is what was echoing in Josiah's mind. After all that Israel had done in not walking in the way of righteousness, Josiah made a covenant with God, and the people made a covenant with God, to walk in His ways. The opposite of taking lawful oaths in His name or making covenants in His name is found in Exodus 20:7, "You shall not take the name of the LORD your God in vain, for the LORD will not hold him guiltless who takes His name in vain." Not taking His name at all or taking His name in vain are two very great sins. This is why membership vows before God and the people of God are very solemn and important in any true church. In fact, some churches have jettisoned the covenant vow before God and the church! They are so worried about pleasing the masses and making church "voluntary" that not only do they not have membership vows, but they have no membership at all. In other words, they have thrown out the crucial point of *covenanting* before God. Membership is simply a formal manner of covenanting with God and the people of God. It is profoundly biblical and utterly necessary if the church desires true biblical reformation.

Josiah, after repentance, gathers the people and places them under a solemn vow, a covenant oath, together, at the

---

[4] *The Westminster Confession of Faith*, 22:1, <u>Of Lawful Oaths and Vows</u>

foundation of the house of God, that they would indeed follow the commandments of God. Such a solemn resolve is the only true catalyst for true biblical reformation. If a man is not held to the task by covenant, then at any time he could simply walk away without any repercussion. He did not promise to anything and he is not held to anything. In churches all across the globe today the solemn setting apart, or covenanting, has been abandoned because failure to uphold the covenant would result in *discipline*, and discipline is not something people want to get involved with because it is too *judgmental*. Keep peace at all costs they say! Churches do not feel safe by vowing to covenant obligations. In essence, keeping the peace is much more important than true biblical reformation because officers in the church cannot be bothered to uphold the Word of God as God intended.

The covenant, or lawful vow, binds the parties to the oath. Without a solemn vow to God in the things of religion people are just full of "talk". It is just *religiosity*. Theology held in the heart must incorporate action. Josiah heard the law read, repented and then made a solemn oath to continue to abide in the commandments of God. There is the pattern. But what is Josiah to do? "...to follow the LORD and to keep His commandments and His testimonies and His statutes." But how? With all his heart and soul! Where has this been stated before? Jesus tells us in Matthew 22:37 that this is the greatest commandment, which are really the tables of the law summarized. It is the recapitulation of Deuteronomy 6:4-6, "Hear, O Israel: The LORD our God, the LORD is one! You shall love the LORD your God with all your heart, with all your soul, and with all your strength. And these words which I command you today shall be in your heart." Can this be any more plain? The church, then, in its desire to follow God and Christ is bound to oath and vow before the living God to fulfill its task. The reality surrounding the greatest commandment to love God with all your heart and mind demonstrates that lawful oaths are *central* to a true confession by any Christian! How could a Christian, truly be on the road of biblical reformation without a solemn resolve, a binding resolve, to uphold the Word of God? He is a hypocrite who thinks he can do so without an oath or vow. He is a pretender (which is what the Greek connotation of what "hypocrite" means). He will never be thorough if he is left to his own whims and desires to how far or long that reformation should go. In fact, he will not even be Christian.

The church must hold and attain the same mindset that Martin Luther had when he stood at the diet of Worms and said, "Here I stand, I can do no other..." Later, this gave way to much of the theology behind the historical landmark of the Augsburg Confession which was read before the Roman Catholic king in absolute opposition to what the king desired. First there is a vow, and then the vow is expanded into practice and action. This is what the church needs today. This is what Josiah did, and every true biblical reformation after him mimicked.

Thirdly, *True biblical Reformation is always a thorough reform.* It is an oxymoron to say "partial reformation". In our passage, Josiah restored *true* worship. It was a thorough cleaning up of the wickedness that went before, to replace it with godliness and true biblical reformation in serving the living God as God so desires. Josiah upheld, upon pain of death as a result of his solemn vow, to uphold the Word of God as God so dictated it from beginning to end. This is holding to an ideal - God's will in worship. In any sanctifying act there must be a hearty resolve to thoroughly reform, or hypocrisy results. That is why the church can never have "sort of" a reformation. It is much like the words of Augustine when he said, "Give me chastity, but not yet." That is akin to, "I want to change, and change a little, but not in every area." Think of the doctrine of repentance – is it just confession of sin? No. It is sight of sin, sorrow for sin, confession of sin, shame of sin, hatred of sin, and turning from sin. It is not just one part. Could Josiah say, "Lord, I want to have right worship, but I am going to skip fixing the temple, or cleaning out the pagan artifacts within it. I am only going to take care of some things, but not all things. I am not resolved to take care of it all, but only some of it." Churches say, "We want biblical worship, but let us add in puppet shows and parades so that we can attract more people to the church and make it entertaining." Religious syncretism of this kind has always been the downfall of the church. Josiah knew this and thoroughly cleansed the land and the temple of everything that God did not require in worship. He even went so far as to clean out their houses as well and remove all the household gods! That is why the principle of worship called the *Regulative Principle* is so important. *God* regulates how worship should be maintained, not men. *God* determines how sinners approach Him, not sinners. Josiah was probably quite afraid of what God would do in the terrible doom to come. Even after finding out what the prophetess said about God's impending judgment, Josiah still thoroughly reformed because that was the right thing to do. Nothing that Josiah did would stop the judgment from coming. But Josiah was blessed not to see it. Instead, regardless of impending doom, the only way to go, after he had heard the words of the Lord, was to thoroughly reform *everything*. Josiah was so thorough, that he dug up that which was unclean (graveyard bones) and had them burned and scattered over all the high places so that they could not be used again. Not only did he destroy those places, but he ensured that they would *never* be raised up again.

How True Biblical Reformation Applies to All Christians Today

Only by the direction of the Word – by a solemn oath to the Word and to God – and with a thorough resolve can true biblical reformation take place. Hypocrisy is completely against true biblical reformation. It is saying with one side of the mouth that one upholds the Bible, and with the other it violates the *Regulative Principle*. That is not reformation – its compromise.

The point of this chapter is to set in motion the ideas that surround true biblical reformation following what God deems the right way of accomplishing it. Josiah is the exemplary picture of how this is to be accomplished. The question to be asked is, "In everything Christians stand for, in everything they covenant with God in, are they resolved to thoroughly follow God's Word no matter where it takes them? Are *you* ready to do that? Remember, the Scottish Commissioners of the Westminster Assembly basically said that without a *Solemn League and Covenant* on their proposed purpose, it would be impossible for them to continue – to reform the church. And so they had Dr. Alexander Henderson draw up a draft of the *Solemn League and Covenant*. But ask searchingly - What was this for? Here is their answer: "THE SOLEMN LEAGUE AND COVENANT, for reformation and defense of religion... and the advancement of the kingdom of our Lord and Saviour JESUS CHRIST...." In other words, they said, "No matter what, we are resolved, *covenanted* to perform this task of reformation." This should be the attitude of every layman, every theologian, every pastor, and every teacher of the church.

The church cannot afford compromising ministers, or bad preaching, or unbiblical worship, or poor theology. Church Covenants binds us together, to a sanctifying reform for the glory of Christ – such covenants press home the reality that Chris-

tians should be like Christ. Josiah typified Jesus Christ – and
Christ in turn loved God so perfectly that the Scripture says,
quoting Psalm 69:9, "...zeal for Your house has eaten me up."
Was Josiah zealous for God's honor and name? Again, 2 Kings
23:25, "Now before him there was no king like him, who turned
to the LORD with all his heart, with all his soul, and with all his
might, according to all the Law of Moses; nor after him did any
arise like him." This is an astounding statement. It is certainly
by grace that Josiah managed this, but the commentator, by
inspiration of the Holy Spirit, makes that remarkable commentary. Was Jesus zealous for God's honor and name? John 2:17,
"Then His disciples remembered that it was written, "Zeal for
Your house has eaten Me up." They could see it in the true biblical reformation that overflowed in his teachings, and actions.
The question then posed is this: Are you zealous for God's hon-
or and name? Will the Holy Spirit consider you like this, "Now
before him there was no Christian like him, who turned to the
LORD with all his heart, with all his soul, and with all his
might, according to all the Law of Moses; nor after him did any
arise like him." May it be that in all you do, that your convic-
tion stands amidst the same kind of powerful covenant with
God as members of His church. Whatever church you attend,
as it so stands within the realm of orthodoxy and the reality of a
true and lawful church, pray that God would help you and all
those therein to uphold the Scriptural law of worship and the
Regulative Principle. Pray that God would help you uphold the
highest standards of godliness in your life, and in the lives of
those Christians around you. Pray also that you would have
true biblical reformation by holding unswervingly to the Word
of God in every area of your life. Such a reformation would be
for the glory of God first, and for the enjoyment of the church
second. But it will only ever be accomplished if you resolve to

accomplish it with all your heart, soul, mind and strength, and with a thorough resolve.

"Whosoever taketh an oath ought duly to consider the weightiness of so solemn an act, and therein to avouch nothing but what he is fully persuaded is the truth (Exodus 20:7; Leviticus 19:12; Jeremiah 4:2; Hosea 10:4): neither may any man bind himself by oath to anything but what is good and just, and what he believeth so to be, and what he is able and resolved to perform (Genesis 24:29; Nehemiah 5:1213; Ecclesiastes 5:2, 5). Yet it is a sin to refuse an oath touching any thing that is good and just, being imposed by lawful authority."

- The Westminster Confession of Faith,
Of Lawful Oaths and Vows, 22:3

2

Careless Living

Jeremiah 7:4, "Do not trust in these lying words, saying, 'The temple of the LORD, the temple of the LORD, the temple of the LORD are these."

People often like to hear what they want to hear, not what they *need* to hear. This applies also to Christians, but unfortunately is of greater consequence when dealing with things that take on or have an eternal significance to them. For example, a hairdresser may say to one of their clients, "I don't like the style you chose and think you should go with another." Now that may be true, and then the client may get upset with the hairdresser and turn to another that would cut hair the way "she" wants. This has little, if any, eternal significance. Hair styles will not damn one or save one. The client may simply choose to hear what they want from another hair dresser that sees things in a different light. Eternal consequences in such things are relatively small. On the other hand, if someone were to tell you that "You are not "doing" religion correctly," or, "the way you meet with God is wrong," such an accusation would have massive ramifications both temporally and eternally. No one wants to hear that the way they "do" religion is wrong, and people certainly believe that their individual experience with God should be just that – an individual experience. However, individual experience does not and cannot dictate how religion should work. Rather, King Jesus determines the manner in which sinners should approach Him. Let the record be set straight – God determines the manner in which sinners are to approach Him, and the Bible was given to His people that they might know the truth on the matter. Only the truth will set men free to worship God rightly, and live before Him in integrity. It is not enough for people to simply hear what they want to hear, rather, they must conform to what God *commands*. God regulates the manner in which sinners are allowed to approach His holy character. He desires to be approached, but in a manner suitable to His nature – in conformity to His standards of holiness.

In the first six chapters of Jeremiah leading up to 7:1-4, the message Jeremiah had been receiving from God was His promise of the coming judgment. If Israel, and Judah, did not repent of their wickedness, they would be sent into exile and punished by God for their sins. However, in contrast to one another, though Israel was exceedingly disobedient in their idolatry, Judah was going to be in for it worse than her sister. Judah was acting more sinful and in a greater intensity than Israel. The first deportation under the conquest of Nebuchadnezzar occurred in 606 B.C. (the one which carried away Daniel). In 597 B.C Jehoiachin revolts and the second deportation involving Judah is seen with the carrying away of Ezekiel as well. The last exile and destruction of Judah is in 586 B.C. where Jerusalem is not only pillaged (as in the second deportation) but also burned, and the temple destroyed. Now looking at Judah, things get much worse.

Jeremiah 7:1-4 is set in the context of occurring twenty years after Josiah's reforms. In other words, this text, which is a hearty rebuke, is set immediately after (about a half of a generation) since the countrywide reform began under Josiah's *co-*

venanted reformation. Follow the picture – only 20 years have passed and sin is taking over. True religion is declining, and God is becoming angry with His people who are not worshipping Him as He desires. Also, at this time, the King of Babylon is Nebuchadnezzar, and the puppet king of Judah is Zedekiah (Mattaniah). Jehoahaz has previously reigned (who was Josiah's son), and was imprisoned by Pharaoh Neco. Jehoahaz did evil in the eyes of the Lord, and then died. Jehoiakim (Josiah's other son) reigned in his place, and also did evil in the eyes of the Lord, and then died. Jehoiakim's son, Jehoiachin, reigns in his place for a very short time, and then is taken captive by Nebuchadnezzar as a slave. His uncle, Mattaniah is made a puppet king and Nebuchadnezzar changes his name to Zedekiah. This is the setting and the terrible sequence of wicked kings who did evil in the eyes of the Lord. The impending judgment is now set upon the people as God told Josiah previously through Huldah the prophetess, and Zedikiah continues to lead the people astray. God, in His longsuffering and wisdom, sent His prophet, Jeremiah, to the people with a message – one of many. But for the purposes of this chapter and the theme of this book, his message has direct bearing on one aspect of how God desires His people to serve Him and not trust in lying words.

Jeremiah comes to the people of Judah with a message of impending judgment. God's promise of the coming judgment reaches back into the previous chapters of Jeremiah. Judah is in for it worse than her sister Israel. Israel has sinned and God brought destruction on them, and Judah is not taking to *heart* the proper object lessons. So God announces that her sin will be worse than the first. In explaining the coming judgment, Jeremiah gives this warning to Judah using Israel as the example. The people rejected Jeremiah's council and the false prophets rose up to tell the people "everything is just fine."

They had already been doing this for a few chapters. In Jeremiah 2:8 the false prophets had been those who sacrificed to Baal. So the charge is brought against them, "The priests did not say, 'Where is the LORD?' And those who handle the law did not know Me; The rulers also transgressed against Me; The prophets prophesied by Baal, And walked after things that do not profit." Instead of turning to God, they turned to idols. And instead of following the Word of God, they mustered up new ways of "pleasing" the people. God calls these men *false prophets,* and they are those who prophesy lies as "blow hards" and "wind bags" (this is the Hebrew meaning behind Jeremiah 5:13). God says, "And the prophets become wind, for the word is not in them. Thus shall it be done to them." Certainly the people had been lead astray. They had not heard God and instead, listened to "hot air".

God is concerned about what His people eat for spiritual food. Feeding the people with lies stands in contrast to what God is doing in feeding the people with righteousness through Jeremiah the prophet. Jeremiah 3:15 places the distinction in glaring view. "And I will give you shepherds according to My heart, who will feed you with knowledge and understanding." Literally this phrase "shepherds who will feed you" is "feeders who will feed you..." These are the heralds of truth. They are the ones that speak what God wants them to speak, and informs the people about what they are suppose to believe, not what they would *like* to believe. In contrast to lies and false prophets, these "feeders" give the people spiritual food that sanctifies them and turns them from wickedness to the truth. Such revelation from God directs people to approach Him properly.

In thinking about the contrast between truth and lies, it would be helpful to look at the exhortation Jeremiah gives, and is instructed to give, in verses 1-4 of chapter 7. In considering Jeremiah's exhortation, the text is set down in this manner:

"The word that came to Jeremiah from the LORD, saying, 2 "Stand in the gate of the LORD's house, and proclaim there this word, and say, 'Hear the word of the LORD, all you of Judah who enter in at these gates to worship the LORD!'" 3 Thus says the LORD of hosts, the God of Israel: "Amend your ways and your doings, and I will cause you to dwell in this place. 4 "Do not trust in these lying words, saying, 'The temple of the LORD, the temple of the LORD, the temple of the LORD are these.'" In verse 1 it says "The word of the LORD..." came to Jeremiah. This is a typical formulation of prophetic speech. In 2 Kings 22-23 Josiah had conformed to the Word of God found written in the book of the Law. Here, God makes a specific declaration through His prophet to deal with the abuses that emerged as a result of living carelessly under those previous reforms. *The Word of the LORD* is coming because after Josiah's reforms, the people went back, whoring after other gods and idols and following lies. God's word should be trusted, and it is this word that comes to Jeremiah and must be delivered to the people.

Then, in verse 2, God tells Jeremiah to stand in the gate, as Josiah did by the pillar, and bring the prophetic word to the worshippers there. "Stand in the gate of the Lord's house..." Literally this means "take your stand, or be planted there." He did not say that Jeremiah was to be planted at "the temple", but literally "Yahweh's habitation." Remember, false prophets have no problem voicing their opinion in the temple as they always have. False teachers love a big crowd of people, and will have no problem going into God's house to speak lies. In contrast, God wants His prophet to stand in His house, in the place where all will hear, and proclaim His Word. This stands in direct opposition to the false teachers. Historically, it may be that the time of this proclamation was during a feast time where all the people, including the false teachers, wayward priests and even the king, would be present. What is Jeremiah to do?

"...proclaim there the Word." In standing in the Lord's house, he would "...proclaim there the Word." The word "proclaim" is the Hebrew Niphal usage meaning "to be proclaimed," or "be read aloud." (It can also have connotations of "summoning," or "to be named.") Jeremiah is to stand in the Lord's House, Yahweh's habitation, most likely the courtyard of the temple, and proclaim the "word" of the Lord. The word "word" is *daw-bar*, which does mean "word," but can also have the idea of holding a "matter or case" against someone. The context seems to set forth the idea of a "case" against the people, and this use is more inclined to translate within this context more appropriately. Here is the idea: there is evidence against the people that needs to be rectified. God is holding this evidence against their wickedness. It was as if God was summoning them to court. He has an air tight case against them and Jeremiah was to proclaim it to them. This fact of having a "case" was all the more stressed to the people since Jeremiah was in the midst of temple as a *priest*. He was representing God before the people as the priest would commonly do in sacrifices, except here, it was by accusing them with an airtight case and calling them to repent in a prophetic role. Remember, previously, the generation before had *covenanted* with God to uphold the book of the Law. Their children forgot the *covenant*. Maybe their parents became careless and did not teach it to them. Whatever may have happened, God's air tight case was to demonstrate the people's sin, and call them to repent. The children have no warrant to cast off what is right and true. But this generation did, and God was angry with them for forsaking right worship and rejecting a right heart.

Verse 2 ends with a direction or object of the message. The message is directed at all "...that enter into these gates to worship the Lord." Were they there to do what the Lord commanded? They were coming to the temple. God had told them to do that. They were worshipping Him, or at least coming to worship. God had told them to do that as well. The problem was that they were not worshipping *rightly*. Again, we see the plague of being religious without having or abiding by the *truth*. They did what they wanted to do in church, not what God wanted them to do. The phrase "worship the Lord" is common throughout the Scriptures, but without a right aim, right doctrine, and a right heart, such "worship" is *meaningless*. Actually, it is repugnant to God, and in this text, God is calling them out on it.

The focus here is on the people collectively, but the message is being delivered to the individuals coming to worship. This is a public call to the people of God to amend their own lives so that each person would then be part of the collective whole, the covenant community, and be worshipping together rightly. Though the covenant community is ultimately in view, if individual people do not do what God desires, it has an impact on the whole camp. For example, there is an individual element as in the case of Achan, who, for a bit gold and nice cloak, brought sin into the camp in Joshua 7:1ff. Achan had transgressed the Law of God, and as a result, the whole camp suffered until it was rectified. The same can be said of Jeremiah 6:20, "To what purpose cometh there to me incense from Sheba, and the sweet cane from a far country? your burnt offerings are not acceptable, nor your sacrifices sweet unto me." These individuals who were coming to worship were not coming *rightly*. Their sacrifices meant nothing to God. And as one sin made the camp unclean until it was rectified (which ultimately came about by the destruction of Achan and his household) then there would be no peace, or righteousness in the midst of the people. So they are called to repent. Take note of this – their sacrifices (their worship with all its ordinances and work) meant nothing to God because they did not come as the Lord has instructed them. Instead they came as they pleased.

Verse 3 begins with "thus says the Lord" again demonstrating the power and truth of the message directly given by God, and then continues with a dictate and rebuke: "Amend your ways and your doings..." The word "amend" here is the Hebrew idea of "do good to," or "deal well with," or "do right." To "amend" something is to make it right or work "righteously," which Jerusalem was not doing. As a matter of fact, they were "doing" quite the opposite. They had sacrificed to false gods and the rulers of the nation, both king and priest, had led them astray. So what does the *covenant* God of a *covenanted* people say to them in rebuke when they break His covenant? What does God wish the covenant people of Judah to know? He wants them to reform! And if they do reform, then the promise stands, "...and I will cause you to dwell in this place." This is a promise based on repentance. Without a thorough change in them, they will not be given the fruit of the promise stated here.

The case against them is exemplified in the failure to keep God's law by God basically telling them, "Do what you said you would do." In sacrificing to other gods, they demonstrated a rejection of the covenant, of God's Word and of God Himself. But, if they repent, and if they do what is right, then God will "settle them down," or settle them to "dwell in this place." The meaning behind this phrase is to have them *established*. Here is a promise based on repentance. If they amend, then God will bless. Yet, in verse 4, God instructs them on how to repent and what they must do to overcome their sin. They are to forget what they have been taught about "religiosity" and instead embrace righteousness.

Verse 4 begins with, "Trust ye not in lying words..." God did not simply tell them to do well, but was specific about *what they should do*. He was pointing out a specific problem. They were trusting in wicked words and now they are to be judged.

Instead, they should be trusting in God's words. Literally the phrase means "to place confidence in..." Even more literally, for this passage, is the idea surrounding "to live carelessly". God does not want them to "trust in lying words" or rather "live carelessly" before Him. God is giving them an opportunity to live well before Him. By trusting in lying words, they were living carelessly before God.

What were these lying words that so utterly shock them off from acting righteously? The text says, "...saying the Temple of the Lord, the Temple of the Lord, the Temple of the Lord...are these." The translation should be "these" not "are these." The text should read, "...saying the Temple of the Lord, the Temple of the Lord, the Temple of the Lord...these." These things mean something. These things are holding great weight. What are "these?" The temple of the Lord is the "these" of the verse. The repetition is placed here as an interpretive help and a warning. Why three times? There are two reasons for this: 1) it is a Hebrew literary device of exclamation. Through the Bible there are places where repetition is used for exclamation. In Isaiah 6 God is "holy, holy, holy." In Genesis 1 it is "there was evening and there was morning". These repetitions are used for exclamation. In the verse at hand, not only is it an exclamation (listen to this or else) but also, 2) this triple threat is referring most likely to the three tiers of the temple; the court, the holy place and holy of holies.   It is used as a *poetic* use of the means of grace hypocritically exploited. The poetry here is a threefold parallel that presses the reader to consider the weight of the rebuke in conjunction to the holy place they are exploiting. The people so trusted in this – *that they had the temple* – they forgot the Words of God and the God who lived in the temple. They lived carelessly before the means of grace. True Biblical Reformation was jettisoned from the life of Israel because they trusted in the "thing" instead of the God of grace behind the "thing." They believed that since God was symbolically in their midst in the temple, they were safe; they were the chosen people, a holy nation. Their argument would revolve around the means instead of the forgiveness attached to the means by the God *of* the means. They "had" the forgiveness of sins in Yom Kippur, the Day of Atonement. They "had" priests to perform religious rituals. They "had" sacrifices to atone for sin. The "had" lots of religious "things." But they did not have the God behind those things. Outward religious visibility is never a sure sign of inward spiritual reality.

God's response to this is ultimately to take away those "things" from them. God has the temple pillaged, then has the temple destroyed. God had initially given them two visual warnings of the reality of their transgressions at two different times over a period of years. They misused the means of grace – in this case the temple, which was their only hope of atonement. Sacrifices are made at the temple. But the people used it as *one means* instead of the *only means*. They were interested in the temple as *part* of their salvation repertoire. It was, to them, more of a heritage instead of the saving means of grace. In this, they included religious syncretism which allowed them to do others "things" instead of just what God commanded them to do. They were blatant idolaters. And on top of that, they did not follow the Word of God and instead followed "lying words." Remember, the king had burned the Word of God written down by Jeremiah and would have rather followed his own dictates, or the dictates of the false prophets, than listen to God's prophet. That is especially significant of the signs of their time. Their idolatry and their departure form the Word of God is especially significant in lessons that modern Christianity could learn from their mistakes.

Lessons We Can Learn From Jeremiah 7:1-4

Doctrine: Carelessly living before the means of grace (outward ritual at the expense of the Word of God) will never maintain or advance inward reformation. This could apply to both the saved and the lost. There is always some benefit to the redeemed elect, the remnant according to grace that remains, though it is even more particular to the lost because they enjoy a form of godliness and deny its power. For instance, going to church is good, but can be done in an evil way through monotony, or through mere duty. But even with the redeemed elect, they can be dissuaded to fall into religious lethargy, and live carelessly before God's ordained means of grace

Theologically, careless living is called apostasy or backsliding. The Christian only has two modes of walking before God – he is either advancing in the things of God, or he is backsliding in the things of God. Practically, this is called "living carelessly." This is exactly what the Israelites did – they lived carelessly before the ordained means of grace, and as a result, overthrew the covenanted reformation Josiah had first set up.

How might one define "careless living?" To "live" means "a state of being." When someone says, "Harry lives like a king," that phrase conjures up ideas of lavish living. When someone says, "Harry is living recklessly," that conjures up the idea of an accident waiting to happen. Living, then, means *someone's existence*, their subsistence, or their very act of breathing from moment to moment. It is their "life." Being "careless" means that they have a reckless disposition of apathy. Think about this sentence: "The doctor was careless while operating on the person's brain." What images does that conjure up? Or what about, "The driver carelessly switched lanes into oncoming traffic." Careless action of any kind demonstrates a lethargic apathy, an uncaring "why do I have to do this again" rote attitude toward a given task. This is what it means to live carelessly.

How might one define "means of grace?" The means of grace are those ordained means which *God defines*, as ways that sinners are to approach Him to receive grace. God says that "this is what you do" and you will receive saving grace or sanctifying grace. That means all those "other" ways are not what God wants His people to do, and are even contrary to what God wants His people to do. The means God gives are the means His people should use – *and none others.*

The means of grace are set in two modes: Saving grace surrounding the Gospel of Jesus Christ, and sanctifying grace surrounds the mortification of sin and the vivification of the new man. In other words, the means of grace surround God's will in how men are saved, and how saved men are sanctified to become more like Jesus Christ according to holiness. The only manner whereby men are saved or sanctified is in Jesus Christ. Jesus Christ is the ordained means by which men must be saved. Acts 4:12 says, "Nor is there salvation in any other, for there is no other name under heaven given among men by which we must be saved." That which points to or directly communicates the way of salvation that God has given in Jesus Christ is what is considered the means of grace. These are means which *are* grace in and of themselves, but also gain saving or sanctifying grace. These means, then, are restricted to God's ordained means found in the ordinances of God. There are no others. For example, there was no temple number "two" in another city that the people could go to. Rather, it was the temple in Jerusalem that God ordained they attend. It would be helpful, then, if salvation and sanctification rest on these limited means, to know *what* they are and *how* Christians should use them.

What are the "means of grace"? These are not just duties performed as if the performance of them will somehow gain Christians acceptability before God. They are not magic "zaps".

One cannot simply read the Bible and thread the words through their eyes. There is more to it than just reading. There is a "power element" to it, which surrounds the power of the Holy Spirit that must be present in order for any action, saving or sanctifying, to be acceptable before God. The instrumental cause of the means of grace is the spiritual operation of the Holy Spirit. This spiritual operation, or empowering, is centered around Jesus Christ and His death and resurrection. In the Old Testament, before the actual death of Christ in time, this properly belonged to the sacrificial system and the temple, performed by the priests for the covenanted community. By faith men trusted in what God had given them as a means to point towards the coming of the Messiah in its types and shadows.

After the death of Christ, this points back to what the Messiah fulfilled and accomplished for the covenanted community of the people of God. So, the means of grace are found primarily, as it always had been found, *in* the Word of God, and the *application* of the Word of God. Old Testament saints look forward to the coming of Christ, and received all the benefits of Christ's work in their time. New Testament saints look back to Christ and receive all the benefits of Christ's work in their time as well.

The Word of God, the self-revelation of God, constitutes the means of grace. Grace may either be found or furthered in such things that contain and exercise God's self revelation. For example, prayer is a means of grace. Prayer is retorting God's word back to God. It is taking the Word of God, forming it into an argument, and sending it back on God again. God listens to His people's prayers, for sure. But God acts in conformity to His Word, and the mind His people are to obtain as "the mind of Christ." 1 Corinthians 2:16 says that, "we have the mind of Christ." What exactly is that mind? The mind of Christ is set in the first part of that verse, 1 Corinthians 2:16 fully says, "For who has known the mind of the LORD that he may instruct Him? But we have the mind of Christ." What, then, is the mind of the Lord? It is the self-revelation of God set down in the Scriptures. If Christians desire to be of "one mind" with God and to "know His will" then following the Word of God is where they start, and end. When Christians pray according to the Word, even when they are aided by the Spirit in this way, it is all according to the Scripture and through the Scripture that such prayers become effectual. Romans 8:27 testifies, "Now He who searches the hearts knows what the mind of the Spirit is, because He makes intercession for the saints according to the will of God." The will of God is that which the Christian should desire to fill his mind up with as Romans 12:2 states, "And do not be conformed to this world, but be transformed by the renewing of your mind, that you may prove what is that good and acceptable and perfect will of God." Where do Christians find this will? Paul connects the practice of the will of God with the Word of God in 2 Timothy 1:1, "Paul, an apostle of Jesus Christ by the will of God, according to the promise of life which is in Christ Jesus." The promises are all "yes and amen" in Christ Jesus who is the Living Word. Standing on the promises of the Word, following the will of God, and being filled with the Living Word are all aspects of prayer. Prayer, as a function of the Word of God, is a means of grace.

Corporate Worship in all its elements is a means of grace. The call to worship, corporate prayer, tithing, the singing of psalms with grace in the heart, the partaking of sacraments, preaching, exhortation, the benediction, all of these are means that are informed and wrapped up in the Word of God. Such worship is to follow the express mandate of God as prescribed in the Scriptures. Men may not, and ought never to inform God as to the manner in which God should be worshipped. Instead, they should, always, *be informed by Him* as to how He so desires worship to be construed as they seek the Word of God. If God has not prescribed choirs in Christian worship, then shame on the church for their choirs. If God has not prescribed altar calls in Christian worship, then shame on the church for their altar calls. If God has not prescribed the use of instruments in Christian worship, then shame on the church for introducing them (circa the 9th century!). If God has not prescribed the use of songs other than the Psalter in Christian worship, then shame on the church for their introduction of uninspired hymns (the first of which was introduced by the heretic Arius in the 4th century!). What did the church do in worship for so many centuries? They followed the Word of God, and follow His prescription for worship.

The proper use of the sacraments are a means of grace, for they are visible signs of the Word of God. *The Westminster Confession of Faith* says, "Sacraments are holy signs and seals of the covenant of grace, immediately instituted by God, to represent Christ, and his benefits; and to confirm our interest in him: as also, to put a visible difference between those that belong unto the church, and the rest of the world; and solemnly to engage them to the service of God in Christ, according to his Word (Romans 4:11; Genesis 17:7, 10, 11; Matthew 28:19; 1 Corinthians 11:23; Romans 6:3-4; Colossians 2:12; 1 Corinthians 10:16; 11:25-26; Galatians 3:27; Exodus 12:48; Genesis 34:14; 1 Corinthians 10:21; Romans 6:3-4; Galatians 3:27; 1 Peter 3:21; 1 Corinthians 5:7-8; 10:16.)"[1]

Experimental and expository Preaching is also a means of grace. *The Directory of Public Worship* says, "Preaching of the word, being the power of God unto salvation, and one of the greatest and most excellent works belonging to the ministry of the gospel, should be so performed, that the workman need not

---

[1] *The Westminster Confession of Faith*, 27:1, Of the Sacraments

be ashamed, but may save himself, and those that hear him."[2] Expository preaching is that preaching which sets forth the meaning or purpose of a passage of Scripture using the grammatical and historical contexts to relay the author's intent to the church. Experimental preaching is concerned to set forth the objective truth of God's Word to bear on the people's hearts. It is, after all, the preacher's desire to see the people moving forward in true biblical reformation of their heart to God. There is also a concern to address the people's experience of the truth under consideration whether it is positive or negative. There is a concern to lead people to an experience of the converting ability of God in regard to that truth. And it is also a discernible intent to motivate them to a greater sanctification. In short, then, the means of grace communicate the realties found in the Word of God through Jesus Christ (the Messiah) to the people of God. Just as God had given the Israelites the temple, so He gives men today the ordained means of grace seen in the same preaching of the word, but men still live carelessly in light of this, of all that surrounds them by means of grace.

If one compares regenerate men with unregenerate men in light of how they use the means of grace, unregenerate men without Jesus Christ (the Messiah) *always* live carelessly before the means of grace. As the initial text primarily demonstrates, men assume that because they have the means of grace that they *will* be saved. This is living carelessly before the means of grace. It is utter folly, and probably one of the greatest of satanic attacks on the blinded mind of men. Some form of religiosity, some form of duty, some attachment to the things of God, in no way qualifies one as *redeemed* by Him. Just because a man goes to church, or he places money in the basket, or he prays, or he attempts doing some good and noble work,

[2] www.apuritansmind.com/PuritanWorship/DirectoryOfPublickWorship.htm

does not, in any way, instantly qualify him for grace. Possession of the *means* does not render a man eligible to obtain the grace that the means *offers*. Think about verse four and the manner Judah was acting. The false prophets were saying, "The Temple of the LORD...." But in reality, the temple was a stumbling block to true grace. Just because a man may buy a bible in the bookstore does not mean that gives him an instantaneous ticket to heaven. God must inwardly and effectually qualify those means in the hearts of men; otherwise men cry out "The temple..." Just as Christ said in John 3:3, "Unless a man is born again he cannot *perceive* the kingdom of heaven." Such men trust in the means and not the God of the means. This is living carelessly before the means of grace.

Non-Christians do not listen to the rebuke, "Trust ye not in lying words..." They trust in the *possibility* of the spiritual reality which becomes carnal, and wicked, and discards the truth of means of grace. It becomes twisted knowledge by the fallen mind and carnal heart. They take that which could be a means to salvation, and strip it of its power. It becomes a duty that they achieve and that they perform, and that they work for, and the spiritual means of grace becomes a carnal medium to satisfy their fallen conscience. Ultimately these kinds of people become exceedingly miserable because there is really nothing going on except a form of carnal habit. There is no transformation, no sanctification, no real attainment of a living relationship with God and Christ. Think of these covenanted priests who had no real spiritual life or vigor, daily performing their duties and thinking, because they had the Temple of the Lord, they were okay. Do you know people like that who attend your church? They have a form of godliness but deny its real power, because *they* become its power. Their rote actions satisfy them. They trust in a false application of the knowledge of the means of grace, and the experience of those means. This is living carelessly before the means of grace.

The Jews knew their duty; they knew what had to be done in the temple - the meticulous obedience to the letter of the law, but they neglected the spirit of the law. What could the Jews have gained if, after they had sacrificed in the temple, they had to go to Baal and worship there? It is what they were doing! Religious men may be exceedingly meticulous about their religiosity, but in doing so forfeit the means of grace. A Christless soul in attending a church service (a great means of grace) could be exceedingly diligent to be on time and take their seat, participate thoroughly in song, take notes diligently, not miss one iota of the sermon, while all the while miss the entire *means of grace*!

On a different note, Christians, sometimes, live carelessly before the means of grace. Make note of this though – even though Christians, truly saved Christians, may backslide, or fall into sin, or misuse the means of grace, the point to be made here is not that they ever lose their salvation, but they do forfeit the sanctifying *affect* of the means of grace. They never forfeit the saving affect in which Christ saved them. However, they can seek after sin, or fall short in a duty, and as a result, miss the sanctification that could have been gained in such an act. There are three ways they do this: First, because Christians have the means of grace they might believe they are automatically sanctified; not saved, but sanctified. Not only are the means of grace accessible – but they have been enlightened to realize this and know this. Saved Israelites, according to God's grace, knew that God wanted them to go to the Temple and to worship in a certain manner. But if they did not worship with their hearts, and in the manner God desired, it was in vain. Worship is not simply a duty; there must be more involved. A minister may visit someone in the hospital that is dying and ill, and may give comfort to the sick, but if the minister says "It was my duty to come here," before he leaves, then the work of the act itself becomes meaningless to the one ministered to (or not ministered to in that case!).

It is unfortunate, but Christians often neglect the means of sanctifying grace. The people of God really know that morning devotions will be a help to their souls, it will edify them, and strengthen them, etc., (and in the past it has done that for them), they know they have been helped by it, and *still* they neglect it. Christians know that the effectual fervent prayer of a righteous man availeth much, but what about the lukewarm lazy prayer? Or are they engaged in the one-minute devotions because *some* is better than *none*?

Being too tired is often a hindrance for good devotions, for prayer meeting, for family devotions, for reading their bible, for bible study, for memorizing verses, etc. Being too busy is often a hindrance for the same. But Christians must remember that they are not automatically sanctified, and when they neglect those means, and then make excuses for those means, they are furthering their dilemma and sin all the more.

Secondly, Christians tend to look at the means as a duty and not as a means to reach their blessed Savior. To use one example, imagine a husband who, for the first time, is away from his wife. He decides, as all good husbands away the first time do, to write a letter to his wife. That letter and the emotions expressed in it, his desires for her, and even his passions for her were written to create a state of eager expectation of meeting again. He cannot wait to be with her again. The Bible, in and of itself, is like reading a love letter sent by Christ to His people. It is not drudgery to read a love letter if one understands the intent of the letter. The Christian should not think of their Bible reading as drudgery, but as a love letter sent to them by Christ. In this way they are impassioned to know Christ more, and to desire Him more. The Shulamite seeks her beloved in the Song of Solomon 5:6, "I opened for my beloved, But my beloved had turned away and was gone. My heart leaped up when he spoke. I sought him, but I could not find him; I called him, but he gave me no answer." The Christian's heart should leap for the Savior. The Christian should seek Him as much as possible. Even if He tarries in His return for a time, the love letter of His word should empower the Christian to be diligent for the Savior and for the cause of the Savior. If the Christian neglects this, that is living carelessly!

Thirdly, careless living will never maintain spiritual vigor, nor will it advance it. If Christians do utilize some of the means of grace, they are content with being a *little* sanctified. It is enough to keep them going but not *growing* – or so they think. What kind of individual reformation of mind and heart is God after? Is He content with a little sanctification in His people? Is He content with a little worship from them? Is a little worship sanctifying enough? The people of Judah had, at least, a *little* sanctification in this regard. Right? They were doing a "little" bit of worship correctly right? No. God says they were trusting in lying words. God says that if the Christian becomes serious about the means He has given them, that He will cause them to "dwell" in His habitation. Remember, this means to "dwell and *continue* to dwell." That means that Christians must serious to seek Christ with all their heart, soul, mind and strength. Christ takes the serious Christian seriously. Those Christians that have a desire to live wholeheartedly before Christ will be, by promise, blessed by God to live in such a manner. And, no doubt, after a single taste of such help, they would never settle for being just a *little* sanctified.

God sees living carelessly before His means of grace as hypocrisy. Some of those things later expressed in Jeremiah 7 are simply a careless attitude to the Law of God. They do not judge rightly; they are oppressing the stranger, fatherless or widow;

they are committing idolatry; they are stealing, murdering, committing adultery, lying, etc. The Christian cannot engage in these things and then come into the house of the Lord and say "God is my God." *God says you cannot do it.*

Inward Reformation (forget Josiah's corporate reformation for a moment) of the individual will never happen when people collectively live carelessly before God. The Christian community cannot maintain their spiritual level nor can they advance it if they live amidst and follow unrighteous teachings, or neglect the ordained means of grace God has given them. One cannot mix going backward in personal reformation with going forward in it. One is either going backward *or* forward. There is never neutrality, or coasting, or monotony in the spiritual walk of the Christian. God will not bless careless living or those who simply cry out "We are in church all the time!" That is akin to saying, "The Temple of the Lord." One must amend their ways, *and then* God will cause them to dwell, or be established in His sanctifying grace. Carelessly living before the means of grace will never maintain or advance inward reformation, rather it will hinder it.

Think about all the characters in the Bible. There are certainly many of them. If you thought of one person in the Bible who was exposed to means of grace more than any other, and threw it all away who would that be? Certainly there could be a few choices made. The people of Judah certainly fit the bill in the text at hand. But even among all the biblical narratives, there is one that stands out among many others, and that is Judas. Think about it - Judas heard all of Christ's sermons. He heard all of Christ's teachings. He slept, walked, talked, ate, and listened in the circle of the twelve apostles. But Judas, among all others, having the means of grace so testified to him, and being a witness to the teachings of Christ Himself, neglected the means of grace and followed the dictates of his wicked heart. He was, of all men, the greatest neglecter of grace that ever lived. Or was he? Christians, when they sin, sin against the blood of Christ. Christ has died for them, and still, they neglect the means whereby they may be more sanctified and made more like the Son of God. And so, who is a greater neglecter of the means of grace? You decide.

Applying Jeremiah's Message to the Contemporary Christian

Five hundred and eighty three years after Judah apostatized and was judged by God, Christ came. It was not until five hundred and eighty three years later that the Jews would have the perfect means of grace given to them visibly, when Jesus Christ was born, and even then, they abused the means by which they would be saved and killed him. They abused God's fullest expression of His love and grace. God prepared a banquet for them in Christ, and they kept right on crying out, "The Temple of the Lord," "The Temple of the Lord," "The Temple of the Lord..." They crucified the only means of grace, and wanted their physical Temple instead. They liked what they did better than what God would have given them in Christ. Religious people have a tendency to abuse the means of grace. And so what is there to say to the Reformed Christian? Three things:

First, with all the wealth of knowledge Reformed Christians have, with the entire heritage in the Reformed Faith, with all the books and all the sermons they have the ability to tap into today, how could they ever become ignorant toward the means of sanctifying grace? What knowledge! The Reformed tradition has the purest expression of the biblical Gospel on the earth in any subsequent age since the coming of Christ. That is why so many link together the *doctrines of grace* for being *Reformed*. The Reformed heritage thrives on the pure, unadulterated Gospel, through God's grace. God has gifted the minds of the greatest preachers, philosophers and theologians in history, and the consensus for good, sound doctrine is formulated in the doctrines of grace. That in turn spawned some of the greatest writings every penned and greatest sermons ever preached.

Then the question arises, why are Reformed Christians today not spiritual giants? Why do Christians need to look *back* in history to find spiritual giants? Why can't Christians look in their own church for those spiritual giants? If Christians do not take time to immerse themselves, with the limited time we have, in studying the Bible and mining its riches and then putting that study into action in their life and worship, that is neglect! How could they ever be tired of the means by which Jesus Christ would sanctify them further? How could they not appreciate the means by which they might become more like Christ? Why is that not their first priority?

Second, with the neglect comes the sin, because Reformed Christians, who hold the Word of God and the Gospel of Jesus Christ in its purest expression, have this tendency to shout out, "I'm Reformed...so I am okay." Why is it that many people see the Reformed Christian as the frozen chosen? They have knowledge, but they do not seem to have a tendency to share it openly, or be as excited and evangelistic as the *Arminian* or *Socinian* or *Liberal* heretic who doesn't have the truth and yet – holds to a zeal without knowledge. The greatest abuse of the means of grace are by those who know those means best – the Reformed Christian. It cannot be argued that the Gospel is most carelessly believed by those who know it the best. Reformation theology can cause Christians to become like the Jews of old. "I'm a Calvinist," and "I'm Reformed..." That is good, but that does not ensure a Christian's growth in Christ. It will not maintain or advance their growth in Christ. Sanctification is only effectual by the operation of the Holy Spirit upon them while partaking of the means of grace with a whole heart. Reformed Christians, then, arguably more than others, should be told to "Amend your ways and doings..."

Reformed Christians, *all* Christians, should be demonstrating a theology put into right practice empowered by the Spirit – *walking* in the Spirit. It is then that all will see true biblical reformation in the mind and hearts as individual Christians, and as a collective unified covenanted community. Mortification of sin and new life in the new man day by day is not won simply by knowledge. It must be knowledge that has been formed into practice and is ignited by the spiritual power of the Spirit of God.

Thirdly, when Christians find themselves saying, "Oh, that was nice", or "Church was okay today," then a red flag should raise up in their spiritual minds that alerts them to the impending danger of the situation. Saying "Prayer was okay," is likened to saying, "The Temple of the Lord." It is like a Christian saying, "I did what I was expected to do today. I got through it." But are they truly saddened at their lack of conforming to Christ? Saying, "I squeezed out devotions in my busy schedule this morning" is the same as saying "The Temple of the Lord." Again - "I did what I was expected to do today. I got through it." Saying, "God understands that the spirit is willing, but the flesh is weak and I'm just a frame made of dust," is coming dangerously close to what Jeremiah said in reaction to that lazy attitude or religiosity of temple worshippers who were content with religiosity. Without taking hold of the means of grace with all of the heart soul mind and strength, Christians will live carelessly before God. They may, in this manner, have the kingdom of God's grace come very close to them, but not *in* them.

The purpose of this chapter was simply to reiterate and press home the realities in Jeremiah 7:4. One text given over and over again was really the substance of this exhortation. Leave this chapter with that in mind. Be reminded of Jere-

miah's rebuke - as one of the redeemed elect, a Reformed
Christian, you fill in the blank, "Trust ye not in lying words saying...I   am   a   Calvinist,   I   am   Reformed,   I   am
_____." May it be that Christians eve-
rywhere would stop living carelessly before the means of grace.

"He who trusteth in Him, that when he shall have been healed inwardly, reformed into a new man, afterwards this mortal flesh too, which doth languish for a time, may in the end itself even recover its most perfect health. Let us therefore be healed for Him. But that we may be healed for Him, let us believe in His right hand."

–*Aurelius Augustine, Sermons on Psalms*

3

Reformation of the Mind

Colossians 3:1-4, "If then you were raised with Christ, seek those things which are above, where Christ is, sitting at the right hand of God. Set your mind on things above, not on things on the earth. For you died, and your life is hidden with Christ in God. When Christ who is our life appears, then you also will appear with Him in glory."

You have probably heard the phrase, "The mind is a terrible thing to waste." This was, in the 1980s, a catch phrase against the war on drugs. However, it could be a campaign among Christians in relationship to Christian doctrine. Doctrine is the cornerstone of the Christian faith. Christ Himself is the eternal *logos* of God, the Word of God, incarnated and expressing the will of the Father. He is the living Word. This revelation is penned down in the words of Scripture so that every Christian may be suited to every good work that God requires of them. If a person is truly converted, as a Christian they have been raised with Christ in His resurrection spiritually. They should, as a result of their new disposition and character, seek those things above that profit their soul. That requires knowledge, and this knowledge is only attained through the propositions of the

Word of God – God's special revelation of Himself to His people. The Apostle Paul, in dealing with this issue of "knowledge"
and "the mind" in relationship to the converted sinner, explains
how the mind should be employed in Colossians 3:1-4, and why
it should be employed in the way he describes. This reformation of the mind is linked very closely to true biblical reformation overall since without the reformation of the mind, there
would never be a reformation of the Christian, and subsequently, there would be no reformation in the church. In this
way, if a mind is wasted on the things of the world instead of
growing by the Word, then truly, the Christian mind is a terrible thing to waste.

Considering Colossians 3

The Christians at Colossae had been shackled by the philosophies of the world, various ceremonies, and types pointing
them to shadows that stand in the background to the full reality
of Christ's work. It is much like talking to someone on a cell
phone, when in fact they live next door and one could simply
walk over and experience their full fellowship. In Colossians
2:16-17 food and drink, new moons, festivals, and shadows of
things to come are mentioned. It seems that novel philosophical views and religious heritage were a stumbling block for
many Christians, and in particular, for the Jewish Christian.
But in taking up these various external forms, they were seen as
additions to the things that are truly necessary found only in
the fulfillments surrounding Christ. These additions are
deemed "self-imposed religion" or will-worship. "Will-
worship" is what Paul referred to as those unnecessary hindrances that take true worship and distort it. Instead of worshipping in the manner that these Jewish Christians wanted on
their own accord, they should have conformed to the worship
that Christ instituted as a result of his life, death and resurrec-

tion. They did not, now, after Christ's-resurrection and ascension, need to entangle themselves with shadows that do not profit. Instead, they simply needed to turn to the principles of Christ's liberating work that freed them from the bondage of external rituals. Old Jewish worship was now obsolete. Not only was it obsolete, but it was a real hindrance to *right* worship now fulfilled under the present intercession of the High Priest in heaven, and under the guidance of the fullness of the Holy Spirit sent by the reigning Messianic King. Christ fulfilled all those ceremonies so that Christians, now, may be lead back to God's will to follow His law with all their *heart*. There is no more need to follow Christ in shadows and types of Him who has *already* come.

In these verses, Paul sets forth a rhetorical question, then a command, reiterates that command, and then gives reasons why Christians should follow that command. He says, "If then you were raised with Christ..." In other words, if this *was* the case, then such should *be* the case. If you were raised with Christ, so then, certain things should follow. It is not "since you have been raised with Christ," but it is an "if" question. The context excludes Paul from simply saying "since you are a born again Christian, you should do certain things." The context demands he deals with people who claim to be delivered (the professing church), but have yet to completely reform their thinking. They are still stuck with earthly ceremonies and vain philosophies and have yet come to realize that they have been utterly delivered from pomp and circumstance of ritualistic works. So the rhetoric runs with an "if" as "if" they are, or "if" they are not. It calls the readers to examine themselves in light of Paul's statement.

When the Christian is crucified with Christ, he is raised with Christ. As the Gospel records, resurrection follows crucifixion. Even after this, though, ascension follows resurrection. Paul is

leading the reader theologically to a certain point. If they were
raised with Christ, then they should be seeking that "raised"
station. So Paul commands them to "seek" something. "Seek
those things which are above." Since Christ is ascended, Paul is
following the line of thought going from the death of Christ
(chapter 1) to the resurrection of Christ (chapter 2) to the ascension of Christ (chapter 3). The command is in the imperative "seek". It is the present active imperative of "all of you
seek", the Greek *zayteyte*.[1] Professing Christians look up to
heaven mentally to find Christ. The Greek word *zaytayow* literally means "to seek in order to find", even to aim at, strive
after or to crave. It carries about it the continual act of seeking
in the active sense. For example, even though Psalm 63:1 is
written in Hebrew, it still gives a good example of the *sense*, "A
Psalm of David when he was in the wilderness of Judah. O God,
You are my God; Early will I seek You; My soul thirsts for You;
My flesh longs for You In a dry and thirsty land Where there is
no water." Thirsting and longing are characteristics of this
sense of "seeking." Hebrews 11:6 also makes this plain, "But
without faith it is impossible to please Him, for he who comes
to God must believe that He is, and that He is a rewarder of
those who diligently seek Him." "Diligently" compliments
"seek." It describes the manner of the seeking, while at the
same time, demonstrates a seeking that should be earnest and
one of great longing. It is not a take it or leave it situation; if a
Christian was raised with Christ then they must be a *Christian
seeker*; if they were not raised with Christ, they do not even
have the ability to seek with intense longing at all. This is not at
all akin to the anti-Christian philosophy of the "seeker movement" surrounding people who "seem to be" seeking salvation
in evangelistic tent revivals. This kind of seeking in the biblical

---

[1] Usually, Greek words should be in *Greek*, not transliterated in English.
However, for ease of readability, I opted to simply use the transliteration.

texts is the kind that Christians, who are already born again, accomplish through the Spirit.

Where are these Christian seekers suppose to seek? The text says, "Where Christ is seated at the right hand of God." This is the object of the Christian's mind. Really, though, it is somewhat of a cryptic saying. Paul's cryptic implication surrounds the question, "what is the aim or goal of the Christian mind?" What is it, exactly, that they are supposed to seek? The verse says, "seek those things which are above where Christ is seated at the right hand of God." Now the question to ask is "What is sought in heaven?" Could it be that Paul desires the Christian mind to seek the throne room of heaven? Certainly, this throne "resides" in heaven and could be one of those things "above where Christ is." What about the saints? They are in heaven as well. What about the glassy sea? Or maybe the angels? All of them are in heaven. But Paul is not speaking of those things. Rather, he is speaking about the power of God in Christ. First, Paul uses the term "Christ." This is a divine title of the Redeemer which means "anointed One." The Christian is to look to the anointed One. Next, the comma is sometimes placed between "is, seated" and this is not present in the Greek text. It becomes more of a hindrance here than a help. Really, the verse should read, "...where *Christ is seated* at the right hand of God." In this, the Christian seeks after the Anointed One of God. The Christian is not bound to the confines this world. He is to look heavenward to the anointed One. Paul is saying - let your whole meditation be as to this: to apply your intellect and your mind to the work of Christ who is sitting at the right hand of God right now and presently interceding on behalf if His saints.

The position and work of Christ that Christians are to set their mind on echoes Psalm 110 and the Covenant of Redemption. Psalm 110:1-5 states, "A Psalm of David. The LORD says to my Lord: "Sit at My right hand until I make Your enemies a footstool for Your feet." The LORD will stretch forth Your strong scepter from Zion, saying, "Rule in the midst of Your enemies." Your people will volunteer freely in the day of Your power; In holy array, from the womb of the dawn, Your youth are to You as the dew. The LORD has sworn and will not change His mind, "You are a priest forever According to the order of Melchizedek." The Lord is at Your right hand; He will shatter kings in the day of His wrath." Paul is teaching in the book of Colossians that these Christians should have *Faith* in Christ, believe in the *Preeminence* of Christ, see clearly the *Reconciliation* of Christ, and continue to have a sacrificial service for Christ. They are not to get entangled with vain philosophy but follow the teachings of Christ. They are not being given over to legalism but follow Christ. They are not to be carnal, worldly-minded or be bound by earthly-mindedness, but keep their eyes focused on Christ! Christ is the "anointed One" who fulfills the Trinitarian pact of faithfulness to the eternal covenant. The eyes, mind, heart and will of the Christian is to be set on Him, and Him alone. He sits at the ultimate and all inclusive place of power – the right hand of God!

Paul presses this idea of the need for Christians to look to Christ at the right hand of God when he repeats himself and says, "Set your minds on the things above, not on things on the earth." This is a positive prescription repeated with a reversal – a negative prescription against "things on the earth." All the ceremonies and shadows of the ceremonial law have been done away with in the sacrifice of Christ, and the Christian's liberty is now set in heaven where Christ is seated, not here upon the earth. Christians should not set themselves on temporary fading shadows, but eternal realities fulfilled in Jesus Christ.

The ceremonial law with all its pomp and circumstance is fulfilled in Christ. That is why Paul makes a differentiation between offerings in the Old Testament and the offering of Christ here, but in conjunction with its benefits to the elect. "For you have died, and your life is hidden with Christ in God." Being dead to the world through Christ's crucifixion, Christians seek life in Christ in heaven, who holds all authority. God is faithful to bring to pass the fullness of blessing in Christ to the believer, but the believer must seek those things above. He cannot be earthbound. Without seeing and understanding this, he will have his mind set on earthly things instead of heavenly things.

In summary then, these professing Christians were having trouble discerning what's important. Various philosophies and Jewish traditions were crowding in to the place where Christ alone should be. If the Christian is truly born again, the Christian mind should be seeking Christ to set his mind on Christ. As a result of dying and being spiritually raised in Christ through His atonement and resurrection victory over death (death which is temporal), the Christian is then to ascend into the heavenlies by way of his mind – his mental thoughts or mediations. They should be set at the hand of power – where Christ is seated at the place of power, the right hand of God – Christ's present Intercession. Paul, then, is expounding the reformation of the mind from that which is bound by carnal duties found in the temporary world, to setting the mind on Christ alone, and His present benefits. If the Christian grasps all this, then the ultimate consolation may ensue – hope in the Redeemer to come.

Lessons Christians Can Learn from the Text

The seeking and setting of the Christian mind on Christ is defined practically as the *reformation of the Christian mind*. To reform the mind is to think rightly about its object and aim. It is to have the mind set in the right spiritual place and thinking about the right spiritual things. The Christian's union with

Christ presses him to have constant spiritual communion with his Savior. Since Christians are freed from the ceremonial law, they must walk more closely with God in Gospel obedience. As heaven and earth are contrary one to the other, both cannot be followed together; and affection to the one will weaken and abate affection to the other. In the Old Testament the elect had to physically go to the place where proper sacrifice would take place – the temple. Today, the Christian simply has to have *right thoughts*. *High thoughts* about God are the Christian's spiritual sacrifice.

It is not that *if* the Christian sets his mind daily on Christ they will die with Christ. It is not a re-dying each day. Working on having thoughts above, or mortifying earthly-mindedness in this way does not gain the dying and raising that Paul speaks about. Rather, since Christians *have* died and *were* raised with Him, Christians *do* this. Their minds are constantly seeking and being set on Christ.

The "mind" is described here instead of the heart (the affections) since active mental reformation can never take place without right *thinking* – yet the Scriptures refer to the mind as the navigating principle of the affections. Passion must never rule the Christian intellect. Instead, the Christian intellect (what it knows about Christ) guides and rules the affections to work biblically.

The Christian cannot have a change of mind (reformation) if he is not *thinking rightly*. To have a mind set on something (whether bad or good doctrine) will involve the affections and the conscience - the whole being. Christ said in Matthew 6:21, "For where your treasure is, there your heart will be also." How does one know what their treasure is? The word "know" is very important. The mind informs the affections and the affections follow the mind. When the affections and passions rule the mind this is the place where the mind falls into disarray. Christians need to listen to Isaiah 26:3, "You keep him in perfect peace whose mind is stayed on you, because he trusts in you." The setting of the mind produces "perfect peace" and in this peace Christians are "kept" by God – kept safe in all they do. Along the same note, Matthew 16:23 gives insight into having a mind set wrongly, on the wrong things, "But he turned and said to Peter, "Get behind me, Satan! You are a hindrance to me. For you are not setting your mind on the things of God, but on the things of man." Instead of setting the mind on the things of God, Peter wanted Christ to hide rather than go down to Jerusalem to die. This was appalling to Christ. Peter was rebuked because he had an earthly, satanic mindset instead of a heavenly mindset.

The Christian should strive to practically fulfill Colossians 3:14 in seeking Christ. Seeking is the mode the Christian walks within. The mode is the command – "seek". The Christian gains an aim through his seeking. The more he seeks Christ the more visible the aim becomes. In the same way, by analogy in *Pilgrim's Progress*, the closer Christian and Hopeful came to the Celestial City in Bunyan's work, the easier it was to see the bright shining light of its countenance on the hill, and subsequently strengthened their endeavor to get there. The mind's employment in earnestly seeking after the "things above" forms a holy aim about itself. Like the sheep walking over and over again to create and fall into a rut, still, the more the sheep walks along the same path, the more defined that path becomes.

The second imperative makes it emphatic; "Set your mind on the things above, not on things on the earth." Here there is repetition again for the purpose of exclamation. The dichotomy is made between things that are eternal over and against things that are temporal. That is why the word "set" is used. "Set" (the Greek *phrownatay*) – "to set in concrete" follows the idea of the sheep's trodden path, or the path in the woods that is clearly defined. If one seeks, ultimately they will set their mind in the right place. Seeking gives birth to setting. They are inseparable. It is not that the mind is instantly there as a result of being raised with Christ. One must persevere which will inevitably bring about active seeking, and that leads to further setting.

Though seeking and setting are vitally important, it is also critically important to seek and set the mind on the pattern of sound words, and not on unorthodox ideas. It is not enough to just set the mind on Jesus, but that Christians should guard very closely *what* Jesus they set to. This "Jesus" cannot be a fabricated Jesus of their own liking, but the one and only true Jesus of the Scriptures. This is nothing other than TRUTH! As Christ said, the *Truth* will set you free. The truth will set men free, or set them at liberty. In other words, *the truth reforms the mind*. Reformation of the mind (and the heart) only occurs by the truth, by a solemn covenanting to uphold the truth, and by a thoroughness of abiding in the truth. Only the truth of God reforms the mind and sets men free.

The mind is to be set in concrete on Christ seated at the right hand of God. Plaster molds are created of footprints at crime scenes. The plaster is poured on the imprint; it hardens, and then "holds" the image of the footprint. In the same way the Word of God should make an imprint on the character of a Christian. Such an imprint should be taken of the things of God and the work of Christ seated at the right hand of God. This means that the mind must be guarded against wickedness and false doctrine, and follow the true Christ of the Scriptures. Christians must make sure to guard their minds from corrupted doctrine and things taught by demons. False doctrine is like gangrene. It rots the mind. Error is idolatry of the mind. Heresy is leprosy of the head. These, the Christian should be aware of in great detail. The Christian should desire, like the plaster, to conform to the image, or print, of Christ. That happens by knowing Christ, and knowing Him through the Word. That is why Paul did not want the Christians at Colossae to be deceived by wrong thinking or some kind of vain religiosity. He wanted their focus on Christ and the truths that surround Him.

Applying these Ideas to the Christian

After surveying these ideas, certainly one can see that it is important to seek and set the mind on Christ, the true Christ of the Scriptures. But then the question comes about, "*How* does the Christian seek and set his mind on Christ?" How does this work practically? This surrounds the work of Christ in the means of grace. Christ has given His church two main conduits to reaching heaven with the mind – the Word and Sacraments. Prayer, bible reading, bible study, church service, the sacraments of baptism and the Lord's Supper, are all means of grace. They are the "means" by which Christ dispenses grace to His people. They are the means God has *ordained* to dispense grace to His people. Christians are, then, to take advantage of them. They have a limited time here on earth (one whole life – however long that is) to use the means God gave them in Christ to see Christ better. Squandering such things would be sin. The setting of the mind is more firmly set through seeking to use the means of grace. Without using the means of grace, the mind will never be set on Christ above.

What if Christians do not set their minds on Christ? If their minds are not set in concrete on Christ, then they are necessarily set on something else. If they are not set on Christ, then they must *necessarily* be set on sundry things of the world. As the apostle assumes, either the Christian's mind is set on Christ above or on the earth below. There is no "in between". Either the Christian is consumed with things temporal or eternal. Earthly minded things are of no eternal value. Why would the Christian waste their mind on them? The heathen of the world that hate Christ are earthly minded. Christians must not disgrace their Savior in this way by removing their mind's eye set on Him, and transfer it to something less worthy (and everything other than Christ is less worthy). This is where Christian often falls into compartmentalized Christianity, or simply holds to the "Sunday Jesus". What is the *Sunday Jesus*? On Sundays they worship God, or think they do, and then the rest of the week they live like devils. However, one cannot love Christ on one day and the world the rest of the days. That is what the Bible calls a *hypocrite*. A hypocrite is one who pretends to get into heaven by deception. The tragedy is that the hypocrite is more deceiving himself than anyone else.

If the mind is the navigating principle of the affections (the convergence of the mind and the heart), then "the Christ" is the navigating principle of the mind. Without a mind set on Christ, Christians give temptations a great foot hold. Sin crouches at the door. If the Christian does not set their mind on Christ then sin walks with them! For those whose mind is not set on Christ, sin is like a bear trap. Animals that are caught in traps that entangle their feet will often gnaw their leg off to escape. It is simply a bloody mess and then ultimately the animal dies as it crawls off in pain. Christians must have the knowledge to avoid the trap or pull the pin and make the trap of no effect. They must never give, for one second, the devil control of their mind. The devil makes the most of every opportunity to ravage and destroy all who have their minds set on Christ. He wants to sift the Christian mind just as he did Peter's mind when he was not thinking about the things of God but the things of men. It is not that the devil wanted Peter to think about the devil – rather, he wanted Peter to think about *earthly things*. And that was Jesus' rebuke to Peter. When he sifts the Christian like Peter, the Christian too will mind earthly things. Remember, Satan has done his job when he has pulled the Christian's mind away from Christ for only a minute, or simply *a second*. In that one second the mind is occupied with things other than giving Christ all the glory.

Those who do not have their minds set on Christ are not of Christ. If the mind is set on the world it is the world's. If it is set on the flesh, it is the flesh's. If it is set on the Devil and sin, then they too own you. Let it never be of the Christian that he is owned of anything other than Christ! The focus is lost when the Christian shifts their mental eyes and looks for something that their brain thinks is "better" than Christ at that moment. Shame will befall every Christian who becomes, by their own choice, earthly minded.

How Colossians 3:1-4 can Practically Change the Christian

The reformation of the mind is the one of the greatest works the Christian can attempt to accomplish by the power of the Spirit. He knows he cannot accomplish this on his own and needs the help of Christ. But the Christian strives to seek and set his mind on that which is most glorious and most beneficial to his walk before the Lord – and that is the person and work of Jesus Christ. Christ came to fulfill His work before the Father so that the entirety of the redeemed Christian would spiritually perceive the glory of the Father in truth. John 17:21-22 says, "that they all may be one, as You, Father, are in Me, and I in You; that they also may be one in Us, that the world may believe that You sent Me. And the glory which You gave Me I have given them, that they may be one just as We are one." The beholding of this glory of the Father, and of Christ, by the Spirit, is accomplished through seeking and setting the mind on the things of God, which is, in a word, the Bible. Seeking things above is not a physical act *as such*, but a mental act. That mental act sends us to heaven to partake of spiritual blessings that are ultimately communicated to us through the Spirit. Christ physically abides in heaven, and here we walk in the Spirit to partake of all the benefits of Christ: communion, love, comfort, consolation, grace, etc. If the mind is not set upon Christ – where all spiritual benefits reside – then the mind becomes self-centered, and earthly minded.

The pursuit of two objects at once spoils both. If a Christian thinks they can have their minds set on Christ and the things of the world at the same time, really, they enjoy neither of them; and thus the vain heart of man by overdoing undoes itself, and reaching at two objects spoils them both. A Christian cannot have their heart torn between heaven and earth for serving two masters is impossible. James 1:8 warns those who have their minds divided, "...he is a double minded man, unstable in all his ways." Double mindedness will never comfort the Christian. It causes doubt, negativity, anxiety, etc. The *reformed mind*, on the other hand, is a mind continually seeking and setting its affections on Jesus Christ – the Almighty God, the Messiah. There in heaven Christ is seated with all power and all benefits of His work ready to dispense them down to the Christian. Christ is ready to pour out His benefits on His body if His church would simply keep their focus on Him and not the things of the world. The world crowds Him out. Rather, Christians should see Him, and Him alone, as sweet and lovely. As the Song of Solomon 5:16 says, "His mouth is most sweet, yes, he is altogether lovely."

Unfortunately, because of the fallen nature of the Christian and the remnants of remaining sin that still need to be mortified and put to death, it is very easy to become earthly minded by the things of the world. Diversions from Christ are easily taken up. For example, the mind will always easily remember stupid things. A person may be in a department store, see a

kaki pair of pants that remind him of an old kaki pair of shorts
he had while in college. That then spurs his mind to think
about some of his college antics, and morally wicked actions,
and then his college "sweetheart." As a result, his illicit relationship spurs his thought processes and he begins to lust after
an event that he should not be thinking about – maybe a lustful
affair. In something as simple as a pair of pants, the mind re-
members stupid things. Any diversion may cause the mind to
wander. Proverbs 27:8 says, "As a bird that wandereth from his
nest, so is a man that wandereth from his place." A man's place
ought to be fixed upon Christ taking every thought captive to
the Scriptures, instead of the world philosophies of self-love,
and self-gratification.

A distraction in the mind becomes a secret sin in the heart.
And this secret sin contracts the guilt and nature of hypocrisy
on a distraction that the Christian should shun. Christ gives a
very clear description of hypocrisy, which agrees very well with
how these distractions become prevalent. He says in Matthew
15:78, "This people draweth nigh unto me with their mouth,
and honoureth me with their lips; but their heart is far from
me." Someone may look as though they are engaged in the task
of setting their mind on Christ, but their heart is not in the task
at hand. They are distracted.

Distractions come in all shapes and sizes. They may be of
things immaterial to good or bad (like a pair of kaki pants) or
something inherently good done at the wrong time (like reading
a good book about the Bible while in church), or something evil
(like lust of any sort). Distractions are conditions, or a particular state of mind, in which the attention is diverted from an
original focus or interest. The mind is often distracted by physical things – things seen. The mind, because it is entertained
with foolish things, files those things away and then recalls at
inopportune times. The Bible calls these kinds of distractions

"idle thoughts". If the Christian's mind is "taken up" with such distractions, and does not fight against them, God may be inclined to give them over to their sin for a time. God may give His people up to their own inventions if they persist in them. God says, "Ephraim is joined to idols; *let him alone*" (Hosea 4:17). It is a very horrible thought to believe that if the Christian continues in a way of sin, God will "let him alone".

Seeking and setting the mind on physical things is easier to focus on because mental seeing, or spiritual understanding, takes real work. The setting of the mind, the reformation of the mind, is really described as continued sanctification, is ultimately accomplished by understanding the truth, not simply seeing a physical object, or having an emotional physical experience. That is why much of Christendom is ignorant of *basic* Christian doctrine. Study and understanding is hard. It takes real work, just like a husband and wife in a marriage, for the bride (the church) to come and know more intimately the Groom (Christ). The Jewish Christians at Colossae were distracted either by 1) philosophies that were more easily manageable in their own minds (much like the popularity surround "the 40 days of purpose" in some of the postmodern church growth ideas), or 2) ceremonies that they could see and experience (much like where churches focus just on "Praise and Worship"). It is easier to focus on that which remains as a form of "religion" without becoming "religiously difficult" in following the commands of Christ. It is easier to sing a song in church, than to go home and study the Bible for an hour.

Christians often become discontent when they focus on circumstances (the temporary) and not Christ (the eternal). A feeling of dissatisfaction and a lack of fulfillment often ensues. Nothing "worldly" can possibly replace the true satisfaction the Christian can find in the gracious power of Christ and His ministry to the soul. People are burned out when they focus on their job, or on their children, or on trying to fill up their day with "stuff", instead of focusing on Christ's will and desire for them to glorify God in all things. Christians become disattached to Christ when we allow their energy to funnel into "things" that are temporal instead of eternal. That is why some of the great biblical maxims instruct Christians to disengage their focus on things that are distracting, and instead "seek first the Kingdom", "grow in grace", "come boldly before the throne", "seek those things above," and the like. Christ's work cannot simply be a compartment of our life, He must be the Christian's "everything."

Certainly, the Christian mind is a terrible thing to waste, and that mind is either a slave to Christ, seeking and setting its affections on Him, or it is a slave to the world. It cannot be a slave to both. It must serve one or the other. The *True Biblical Reformation* of the mind will never occur if the mind is not set upon Christ. Christ must be the practical Lord of the Christian's mind. Not simply a puppet king who is part of the Christian mind on Sunday mornings for the sake of convenience. Christ is not there to satiate a religious feeling of guilt. He is the King, the Lord of Glory, which commands His people to love Him with their entire mind.

"Nothing should be used in the Church which has not either the express Word of God to support it, or otherwise is a thing indifferent in itself which brings no profit when done or used, but no harm when not done or omitted."

– Dr. John Hooper, The Regulative Principle and Things
Indifferent

Reformation of our Worship

John 4:1-26, "Therefore, when the Lord knew that the Pharisees had heard that Jesus made and baptized more disciples
than John ² (though Jesus Himself did not baptize, but His disciples), ³ He left Judea and departed again to Galilee. ⁴ But He
needed to go through Samaria. ⁵ So He came to a city of Samaria which is called Sychar, near the plot of ground that Jacob
gave to his son Joseph. ⁶ Now Jacob's well was there. Jesus
therefore, being wearied from His journey, sat thus by the well.
It was about the sixth hour. ⁷ A woman of Samaria came to
draw water. Jesus said to her, "Give Me a drink." ⁸ For His disciples had gone away into the city to buy food. ⁹ Then the
woman of Samaria said to Him, "How is it that You, being a
Jew, ask a drink from me, a Samaritan woman?" For Jews have
no dealings with Samaritans. ¹⁰ Jesus answered and said to her,
"If you knew the gift of God, and who it is who says to you, 'Give
Me a drink,' you would have asked Him, and He would have
given you living water." ¹¹ The woman said to Him, "Sir, You
have nothing to draw with, and the well is deep. Where then do
You get that living water? ¹² "Are You greater than our father
Jacob, who gave us the well, and drank from it himself, as well

as his sons and his livestock?" ¹³ Jesus answered and said to her, "Whoever drinks of this water will thirst again, ¹⁴ "but whoever drinks of the water that I shall give him will never thirst. But the water that I shall give him will become in him a fountain of water springing up into everlasting life." ¹⁵ The woman said to Him, "Sir, give me this water, that I may not thirst, nor come here to draw." ¹⁶ Jesus said to her, "Go, call your husband, and come here." ¹⁷ The woman answered and said, "I have no husband." Jesus said to her, "You have well said, 'I have no husband,' ¹⁸ "for you have had five husbands, and the one whom you now have is not your husband; in that you spoke truly." ¹⁹ The woman said to Him, "Sir, I perceive that You are a prophet. ²⁰ "Our fathers worshiped on this mountain, and you Jews say that in Jerusalem is the place where one ought to worship." ²¹ Jesus said to her, "Woman, believe Me, the hour is coming when you will neither on this mountain, nor in Jerusalem, worship the Father. ²² "You worship what you do not know; we know what we worship, for salvation is of the Jews. ²³ "But the hour is coming, and now is, when the true worshipers will worship the Father in spirit and truth; for the Father is seeking such to worship Him. ²⁴ "God is Spirit, and those who worship Him must worship in spirit and truth." ²⁵ The woman said to Him, "I know that Messiah is coming" (who is called Christ). "When He comes, He will tell us all things." ²⁶ Jesus said to her, "I who speak to you am He."

In this chapter, we are going to deal with the text of John 4 in sections. Instead of simply quoting and commenting on the text, we will deal with it piece by piece. It is one of the most beloved passages of Christ's interaction with sinners.

In demonstrating the truth of the Messiah and His divinity, the apostle John, being carried along by the Holy Spirit, thought it prudent to add this amazing passage of the Jewish Messiah and his dealings with a *Samaritan* woman. Though

Christ has said that He came for the lost tribes of Israel (Matthew 15:24), He takes many opportunities throughout the Gospels to deal with the common symptom of the fall that needs God's grace – spiritual blindness. Having corrected Nicodemas in John chapter 3 on spiritual birth, and true belief, John solidifies such a teaching in his Gospel with demonstrating the practical outworking of the regenerating grace of God in chapter 4. And who is best to demonstrate the power of God that reaches across national lines than a Samaritan *woman*?

The text begins with John 4:1-2, "Therefore, when the Lord knew that the Pharisees had heard that Jesus made and baptized more disciples than John (though Jesus Himself did not baptize, but His disciples)..." From the viewpoint of the Pharisees things were getting worse and not better. John the Baptist had baptized, and Jesus' disciples were baptizing more. Converts were being made and this is not good for the anti-Christian Jewish system. Jesus' "kingdom" was growing, and their "kingdom" was diminishing. Since they were more interested in their own version of God's kingdom, Christ was a real threat, even worse than the work that John had previously accomplished in calling men to repentance.

In John 4:3-6 it continues, "He left Judea and departed again to Galilee. But He needed to go through Samaria. So He came to a city of Samaria which is called Sychar, near the plot of ground that Jacob gave to his son Joseph. Now Jacob's well was there. Jesus therefore, being wearied from His journey, sat thus by the well. It was about the sixth hour." The calamity that could have befell Christ before His appointed time was of concern, so He left the area. He went back again to Galilee, where He previously performed the change of the water into wine. He "had to go" finding the shortest route to His destination, and He passed through Samaria. There He moves through a town called Sychar where Jacob had given his son Joseph the plot of land, and where Joseph was ultimately buried. (cf. Genesis 48:22 and Genesis 50:25-26). This is where Jacob's spring is found. Jacob, in his day, wanted his own well so that he would have little problems watering his flocks and not have problems with surrounding neighbors (Genesis 26:15). Jesus was tired, and thirsty, and it was about the time (the sixth hour) when people would come to this well and draw water.

John 4:7-10 continues the narrative, "A woman of Samaria came to draw water. Jesus said to her, "Give Me a drink." For His disciples had gone away into the city to buy food. Then the woman of Samaria said to Him, "How is it that You, being a Jew, ask a drink from me, a Samaritan woman?" For Jews have no dealings with Samaritans. Jesus answered and said to her, "If you knew the gift of God, and who it is who says to you, 'Give Me a drink,' you would have asked Him, and He would have given you living water." Here, the Lord sees the opportunity to not only win over this Samaritan woman, but also her neighbors, which happens later in the passage. Jesus, in bringing the true Kingdom of God to her front door, first uses *her* compassion and asks her for a drink. She responds, not with a drink, but by bringing up the animosity between Jews and Samaritans. How can a Jew talk to a Samaritan, much less a Samaritan woman! Historically there is a reason which requires some explanation. Israel's last king Hosea, after yielding to Assyria, transferred allegiance to Egypt. Samaria, the capital of the northern Kingdom, was surrounded by Shalmaneser and was finally taken by Sargon in 722 BC. (cf. 2 Kings 17:36). Most of the people were driven out and carried away to Assyria. The very poor were allowed to stay. Foreigners from Babylon were brought into this region and intermarried with the Israelites. This mixed population was called Samaritans, after the capital city of Samaria. These "Israelites" asked the king for an Israelite priest to be brought back to teach them the law because they knew they had displeased God. But this basically became a religious synchronic mess, and paganism and Judaism mixed together to form an aberration of the truth of God's covenant people. When the Jews returned from Babylon in 586 BC, the Samaritans wanted to come back as well and help rebuild the city and temple, but the Jews refused. Thus, the Samaritans hated the Jews and built their own temple to worship at on Gerazim. Notice in this summary, that *religion* itself *changed* with the shift of *cultural* influence.

Samaritans "have no dealings" with Jews. Jews were not allowed to relate to the Samaritans (at least this is how the Jews thought) according to laws of purity (cf. Leviticus 15) or even to drink with them. Instead of rejecting the discussion, Jesus not only asks for a drink, but enflames her curiosity with a riddle of sorts, and tells her that she should ask *Him* for living water. As Nicodemus, the Jew, in John chapter 3 did not understand being *born again*, so Jesus with a Samaritan woman now gives her a riddle about *living water*. Jesus rebukes her with a rebuke where He says "If you knew...," which means she *did not* know. She did not immediately give Him water when He asked. However, if she would have *asked Him* for living water, He would have given it *immediately*.

John continues in another "round" between the woman and Christ in John 4:11-15 when the woman asks, "The woman said to Him, "Sir, You have nothing to draw with, and the well is deep. Where then do You get that living water? "Are You greater than our father Jacob, who gave us the well, and drank from it himself, as well as his sons and his livestock?" Jesus answered and said to her, "Whoever drinks of this water will thirst again, "but whoever drinks of the water that I shall give him will never thirst. But the water that I shall give him will become in him a fountain of water springing up into everlasting life." The woman said to Him, "Sir, give me this water, that I may not thirst, nor come here to draw." She asks if He is greater than Jacob. He responds by telling her He is, by an explanation of living water. People come to Jacob's well and they continually thirst. Those that come to Jesus to drink living water will never thirst. Then the Samaritan woman wants this water. Jesus asked her for a drink, *she now asks Him for living water.*

In John 4:16-22 Jesus responds with a seemingly strange reply that appears to not fit into the conversation when he says to her, "Jesus said to her, "Go, call your husband, and come here." The woman answered and said, "I have no husband." Jesus said to her, "You have well said, 'I have no husband,' "for you have had five husbands, and the one whom you now have is not your husband; in that you spoke truly." The woman said to Him, "Sir, I perceive that You are a prophet. "Our fathers worshiped on this mountain, and you Jews say that in Jerusalem is the place where one ought to worship." Jesus said to her, "Woman, believe Me, the hour is coming when you will neither on this mountain, nor in Jerusalem, worship the Father." You worship what you do not know; we know what we worship, for salvation is of the Jews." Now, the Samaritan woman wants water, but Jesus asks her about her *ethics.* Why? It seemed that Christ, according to the previous verses, would have given here the water immediately. Did He not say He would give it to her immediately? But Jesus knows that she cannot have living water without a sense of her guilt. Living water, salvation, will not matter to those who are not sensible of their guilt before God. Thus, Jesus attacks her ethics.

The Samaritan woman says that she does not have a husband. She was talkative before. In the previous verses she used many words to answer and ask questions as the Greek text demonstrates. Here she uses just three words. The woman is living with a man. She has had five other husbands. She then perceives that Jesus is a prophet because He is telling her things only the Omniscient God could know. It did not seem to be common knowledge; otherwise she would not have cared about those questions which everyone would have known. Later on, as John records, she will go back to the town and tell everyone that Jesus has explained her entire life.

She then talks about worship because the coming Messiah will teach everyone how to worship correctly. Note that she never denies her guilt. Where should people worship? She notices that Jesus is a prophet, and that He is a Jewish Prophet. She probably picked that up as a result of Jesus' accent. She figures that Christ will now tell her to amend her life and ways, yet, that would take going to the temple – but which temple? That means she would have to have a place to worship. Would it have been at Mt. Gerazim, or would it be in Jerusalem? Jesus replies that exclusivity of worship is coming to an end. Worship will not be tied to a locale after the finished work of the Messiah. Jesus instructs her that she worships what she does not know – for the Samaritans rejected the prophetical and poetic books of the Old Testament, but the Jews accept all the books of the Old Testament and that informs them as to who God is – they worship what they know. "The salvation" is from the Jews, not from partial truth. Christ is not only demonstrating her need for salvation, but also for amending her life and the need to worship rightly by the truth of God.

In John 4:23-26 there is a pre-climax to the passage with the woman. The text reads, "But the hour is coming, and now is, when the true worshipers will worship the Father in spirit and truth; for the Father is seeking such to worship Him." God is Spirit, and those who worship Him must worship in spirit and truth." The woman said to Him, "I know that Messiah is coming" (who is called Christ). "When He comes, He will tell us all things." Jesus said to her, "I who speak to you am He." The hour is coming; it is *now* and not *yet*. The ceremonial law will

soon be utterly done away with, the temple veil torn, and true
worshippers will not worship by location, or by the physical
alone. This is how Jesus presses home the nature of Kingdom
worship. Reformation is about to take place. In fact, it is taking place in her midst. The verb "will worship" means "to respect." True worshippers respect God. The context determines, then how one should translate "spirit and truth." Jesus
has demonstrated two key points here: 1) physical considerations will no longer be considered, and 2) true worship must be
done in truth as the Messiah dictates, which is by special revelation (not rejecting any of the Scriptures as the Samaritans
had).

What particularly does Jesus mean when he says, "spirit
and truth?" The Father is to be worshipped, and He is seeking
true worshippers to *worship* Him in a peculiar manner. They
are to worship "in spirit and truth." The necessity of spiritual
worship, according to Jesus, is because God is a Spirit. Not only will they worship God but they cannot worship God any other
way but by spirit and truth. This is done not only "in the Spirit"
but by "spirit and truth" – by the entirety of a man's redeemed
humanity, and by the truth of special revelation. This is true
heart worship that is completely informed by God's Word, not
by part of God's Word.

Next, Jesus corrects her on the timing of the Messiah. The
Messiah is coming she says, and when He comes He will explain everything. Jesus says to her (not to the Pharisees who
would have certainly condemned Him) that He is the Messiah.
By His death, the sacrifice for His elect people, Christ is reforming worship. He is changing worship that is tied to ritual, and
replacing it with worship in the fullness of being, and solely by
the truth of God. The ceremonial law is being abrogated and
outward object lessons will no longer be needed. The Messiah
will come and institute worship that is done in the entirety of

the redeemed person, and by the truth. This is what the Samaritan woman needed to learn from the Messiah.

What Is This Text Principally Teaching?

God must be worshipped with the entirety of a Christian's redeemed humanity, and only by the truth of His Word. What does it mean to worship with "the entirety of a Christian's redeemed humanity?" Whether one looks in the Old Testament or the New Testament they will find God looking to men to worship with a right heart – a heart after true biblical reformation. For example, Psalm 51:16 says, "For You do not desire sacrifice, or else I would give it; You do not delight in burnt offering." 1 Samuel 15:22 says, "Then Samuel said: "Has the LORD as great delight in burnt offerings and sacrifices, as in obeying the voice of the LORD? Behold, to obey is better than sacrifice, And to heed than the fat of rams." But Jesus did not say "spirit" simply to enforce the idea that men must worship God with their whole heart, soul, mind and strength. Rather, it also houses a "now and not yet" concept. For the Samaritan woman, worship *is* now, but it will be *more* revealed in the death of Christ. When Jesus says "the hour is coming..." He is referring to the tearing of the veil, and the displacement of the temples – whether in Samaria or in Jerusalem. Being tied to a specific locality is not the point. Through Christ, the entirety of the Christian's redeemed being will worship God, not by attaching themselves to a physical place, but solely by His offering and the Christian's connection *to Him*. He is the One who gives rivers of living water to those the Father is seeking to worship Him in spirit and truth. These Christians never thirst, and they are completely satisfied in Him. This echoes the same understanding of Christ's point in Matthew 22:37, "Jesus said to him, "You shall love the LORD your God with all your heart, with all your soul, and with all your mind."

Jesus also pointed out in that narrative that it is by special revelation that Christian's worship the Father. Jesus rejected the Samaritan concept of worshiping in ignorance without the Word. It is utterly impossible to worship God rightly while remaining in ignorance. Christ told her that she worshipped a God she did not know because she, and all Samaritans, rejected much of the Scriptures, the Old Testament! The Old Testament, specifically the Septuagint, was the Bible Christ used! Thus, to eliminate huge portions of it would be an offense to Christ. This is important because 1) men cannot invent their own ways or ideas into the worship of the church, and 2) ignorance of what to do is as bad as not doing what worshippers ought to do. A shift or change in culture had grievously affected these Samaritans because Babylonian paganism had infiltrated their worship through intermarriage. As a result, the Samaritans had been paying for that sin for generations. They were worshiping, but they were worshipping incorrectly, and ignorantly. Christ commands that they must worship in spirit and the truth.

Christians must be reminded that shifts in contemporary culture may never dictate the manner in which God's people worship Him. Samaria was the worse for its cultural shift. For hundreds of years they rejected God's truth, and worshipped a God they did not even know. Deuteronomy 15:21 poignantly says, "But if there is a defect in it, if it is lame or blind or has any serious defect, you shall not sacrifice it to the LORD your God." Malachi 1:8 echoes this, "And when you offer the blind as a sacrifice, Is it not evil? And when you offer the lame and sick, Is it not evil?" And Hosea 4:6 clinches this concept, "My people are destroyed for lack of knowledge. Because you have rejected knowledge, I also will reject you from being priest for Me; Because you have forgotten the law of your God, I also will forget your children."

Christians should read in awe that Christ took the time to witness to a Samaritan. This shows His great compassion – even tough love – to rescue His elect to become *Father seekers*. Contemporary culture ought not, cannot, dictate religion. Men have no option but to worship God in spirit and truth. If the 21st century church took hold of that idea alone – all the vanity of will-worship (self imposed worship) would be utterly destroyed and forsaken.

If something changes in culture, this does not necessitate that the Christian religion and worship of God should shift one *iota*. Keeping up with the Joneses is not a Biblical idea. Instead, true religion should arrest that culture from moving in the wrong direction.

Follow this line of thinking: Culture would have never elected Theodore Roosevelt if he ran today. Today it is not a sociopolitical agenda that wins elections, but rather "image." In other words, as politically incorrect as it sounds, it is not "American" to vote for a cripple. Presidents do not *look like* cripples. In this way the modern media does not *throw away* thoughtfulness to an ideal, rather it simply *displaces* it. People measure a culture by what it deems or sees as *significant*. When a culture that thrives on triviality deems a medium, like television which is filled with junk, to be a significant source of information, and people believe it, there is a great problem. Reader, ask yourself, when was the last time you have watched TV or heard the radio or even read the morning newspaper and you changed your plans for the day, or those issues helped you resolve an issue you were working on? Never?

Television, to continue the example, has become the main 21st century medium of philosophical teaching. It is what propagates information in high volume and raises "intelligence" to what it propagates. Intelligence is defined as *the ability to grasp the truth of thing*. But if the country is being immersed, for example, in the philosophical medium of triviality, then the very act of simply "considering something" or being "thoughtful" about something is hard (even exceedingly difficult) because people are being conditioned by culture to *not think* and simply *experience* the feelings and emotion of good entertainment. Neil Postman, in his excellent survey of American culture called *Amusing Ourselves to Death*, says, "We might even say that America was founded by Intellectuals, from which it has taken two centuries and a communications revolution to recover."[1]

It used to be the case when people could sit and listen to a lecture for seven hours, but with our 21st century media shift to pictures, the mind can only handle a 45 minute sermon before it almost implodes. The media has shifted culture and has given a brand new meaning to the way people learn – by sight and not by thought. This has *affected* thought. American no longer talks to one another, they *entertain* one another. Even news is packaged as *entertainment*. Ultimately the children of our age will not be able to read a book because it is simply not exciting enough as watching a three hour movie. Sesame Street, for example, does not teach children to love school, or reading, or education. Rather, it teaches them to love *television*.

Where does Christ stand on this? First, culture shifts, then media shifts (the manner of transmitting information), the individual's mind shifts, and then guess what else is affected? The medium that God has ordained for the salvation of His elect and their sanctification is the truth of the Word, preached, and partaken in the Sacraments. When the medium of transmission changes, the practical impact of the Word and Sacraments is affect – they *change and shift*. Will *worship*, then, be affected? Will Samaria happen all over again? How will a media savvy culture adapt religion to itself? Generally our techno-

---

[1] Neil Postman, *Amusing Ourselves to Death*, 41.

logical age does not say "never listen to sermons," or, "Don't partake of the sacraments." Instead, 21st century professing Christians decide that new inventions that attract unchurched Harry and Sally will be *more* affective in a *culture* saturated with the media than simply the truth. The worship of the Father, then, becomes profoundly affected for the worse because the worshippers the Father is seeking are suppose to be worshipping Him in spirit and truth, but instead, they are searching for an emotional or ecstatic experience since they have forgotten how to think, and how to acquire knowledge – the only means of knowing about salvation.

People are emotional. God designed them that way. But their emotions should be guided by their right *thinking*. People can cry by listening to the National Anthem if the right situation is in order – a talented singer, the right camera angle, the right night, the right stadium, etc. People are looking for "Praise and Worship" in church, not the *God* of worship. People that are looking for "dynamic" praise and worship are never going to find it in Reformed Liturgy. Think about what Christ said – the Father is seeking worshippers who worship in spirit and truth. How central is that? There is no other kind of worship. Worship that adapts to culture is not worship in spirit and truth. It is not worship the Father is seeking.

Martin Luther said, "Even so there is today in the churches a great ringing of bells, blowing of trumpets, singing, shouting, and intoning, yet I fear precious little worship of God, Who would be worshiped in spirit and in truth, as He says in John 4:24." John Calvin, in His work, *The Necessity of Reforming the Church,* said that worship is "the central focus" of the Christian. John Owen stated, "But things are indeed quite otherwise: "God is a Spirit, and will be worshipped in spirit and in truth," John 4:24. And no devotion is acceptable unto him, but what proceedeth from and is an effect of faith; for "without faith it is impossible to please God." If there is no truth, then there is, subsequently, no real faith. This leads us to the inevitable conclusion, that most of the American church has simply fallen headlong into a religious formalism.

A common mistake in the affects of contemporary shifts in culture is confusing worship for evangelism. Corporate worship is for Father seekers – true, regenerated Christians who love the truth, and the God of truth. Worship dictates a certain response to the realities held in the truth. For some reason, people want to respond to God today like they do at a rock concert or football game. The "Praise and Worship" leader's job is to whip up the troops. However, Jesus said that truth in this manner is a response to the Word and Sacraments. Worship is corporate and not individual in this regard. It is not about the individual's feelings and emotions, but the response as a *corporate* entity. Worship is not only an individual's experience, but a corporate response of the covenant community to the Word and Sacraments. Individuals partake of these means, but they respond and worship as a corporate body, and not simply as individuals at church. This has profound affects on the manner of worship, the mode of worship, the object of worship – *everything* in worship.

God has condemned and forbidden fabricated worship. Oftentimes, evangelical churches reshape worship and repackage it to manipulate the congregation into a "worship experience". Worship in a given church always reflects what people think about God. Jesus says worship only exists when it is fueled by the truth. And yet people are looking for an emotional experience solely on the basis that they think such a connection of *feeling* is pleasing to the Father. Older forms of worship are deemed traditional, newer forms are contemporary Praise and Worship. Advocates of Praise and Worship really want a limited amount of simple and spiritually empty emotionalism that can be found in mantra like ditties that have evolved from the 70's charismatic movement. They want entertainment because they live in an entertaining age. What would an average American church say to singing the Psalter alone (the 150 psalms) and to tossing the liturgical dances, the puppet shows, the skits, and the like? They would say a church that discarded man-made worship (all those entertaining facets) to simply sing the Psalms is going to die a quick death. They will say "That kind of old school worship will never work in today's culture because people do not like it." Does it really matter, though, what people like or want? They will say, "yes, if you care about how big your church is." Christ, however, founded His church on the Psalter. But contemporary Christendom desires "entertainment therapy"! People think they have worshipped God after an hour of Praise and Worship, and really, they have been culturally conditioned to worship their emotions instead of God. The world of entertainment and media has touched the 21st century mind and offered it a fabricated fantasy inviting them to compare the Church with its excitement. Evil is *boredom*, and that is remedied with far greater ease than sin. It is remedied not by Christ, but by a cable hookup for digital cable in your home, and a bouncing ball to follow on Sunday Morning on the big screen for *Praise and Worship.*

True Biblical Reformation and its worship, though, functions according to the premise that worship should never be novel and creative, but routine, regular and repetitious. Remember, Jesus did not say "evolving truth" but "*the* truth." Ask any Israelite what was going to happen on Yom Kippur and it would never have involved anything but what God had commanded them. They were not going to be surprised with a new song to sing, or a new way to cut up the lamb or goat. It was rote, and expected, but still *heart* worship informed by what they knew about God and what God commanded them to accomplish in the act of worship. Contemporary evangelicals are trying to be novel and creative so "tithers" do not fall into a rut on Sundays. Television shows that fall into ruts are canceled. People will not come to something that does not entertain them. The nighttime entertainment guru that thrives on novelty, triviality and disseminating useless information, David Letterman, even deemed that kind of idea as "infotainment." Such infotainment simply distracts the attention of the worshipper on what actually matters - the truth. This, it should be evident at this stage that cultural shifts are never allowed to inform Biblical Worship or Religion. Will people, then, be guided by the novelty of infotainment, or by the truth? What do they really want?

How Does this Affect Worship and Church Practically?

As a worshipper of First Church "wherever", how would you explain to others the character of your Church? This is a critical question for a church that is trying to reform for the glory of God.

The Church is primarily there to equip the worshipper to worship the Father as a "Father seeker" who worships in spirit and truth.

That is primary. It is *central*. Jesus explains that the evangelical pastor is not suppose to be the CEO, is not suppose to be a psychologist in the pulpit, and he is not suppose to engineer good relations and warm feelings. Instead, it should be founded on spirit (the entirety of the Christian's redeemed humanity in worship) and truth (dictated by special revelation and not by culture). Reader, you might say, "I think of our church in that way. Spirit and truth, that's what I'm there for." But when you "advertise" to the community, what mode or method do you use? The church down the way will say "free food on Sunday", or "picnic next Sunday– all invited". Once a year a group comes down to have "Beachfest" where there are face painting, hotdogs, cookouts, skits, music, and oh, yes, something will be "shared" from the pulpit as well. When you reach out to the neighborhood, how do you form your "advertising"? Is your church taken captive by the deception that culture should dictate how you form your message and appeal to the "needs" of the community, or will it be informed by the biblical message of spirit and truth, and worship? Will your church think about how it will win over a visitor by appealing to what they need, or what God wants? This is very relevant to the message of any Church anywhere. For Jesus, His method was to bridge the hostile gap, explain the Father's desire, demonstrate the sinner's guilt, and offer living water to the shameful. Could your church advertise this way: "Church desires wicked, guilty sinners to seek God the Father in worship"? Will that "sell"? The question, "Will that sell", is an effect that culture has on the church at large. Did the reformers, when they were reforming worship, say, "This whole "reformation" thing – *do you think this will sell?*" Not at all. But for church marketers, the *audience* is sovereign and ideas find legitimacy and value only within the *marketplace*. That is the inevitable result of marketing the church instead of gathering Father seekers who worship in spirit and truth.

How should others outside the Church perceive Your Church? Americans are individualists, and they are conformists. Not only does this permeate society, but it permeates American Christian Theology. It is more particularly called relativism and pragmatism.

Most people out there think that the pastor in a church is supposed to simply be a good friend to everyone. They think that worship should meet felt needs and be culturally relevant for the "on-the-go American". Pastors are those men who shake people's hands in the morning, and say "How do you do?"[2] His job mainly consists of "keeping the sheep happy." In contemporary Christendom, people are *managed* in Churches. Rather, churches should look different and act different than large corporations do in the world. People outside looking in should say, "Why are they so different?" and ,"Why are they not following the Evangelical Crowd?"   But, this will affect the overall attendance of a church and thus, numbers will decreases because church is not relative. Yet God still expects His people to act a certain way – like Christians – not like the world.

What do you want your church to be? A Reforming church is radically an off-centered church from the cultural norm. What will your response be and your actions be in the way you market your church to your friends and neighbors? Is "market" even the right word? Think through the implications of the church that follows the world - that the presence of the Evangelical Mega Church has barely caused a theological ripple in worship of the American church, or among the Country itself, for over 200 years. Is your church one of them? Church, instead, must never turn from dependence on God as those the Father seeks to worship Him, to management of God which is characteristic of Evangelicalism across the world. It is the marketability of God that a true church has to deal with against the grain of modern society. You can instantly tell where your mind is at from the last time you spoke with someone about your church. Did you tell them about the worship team and youth group, or the preaching of the Word and administration

---

[2] This writer has seen firsthand in various churches the insistence of "shaking everyone's hands" as a preliminary attestation for whether or not a man is fit for the ministry. No, this is not a joke. A ministerial candidate in one particular church this writer attended for some years, was excused from the "running" because he did not display the charismatic charm of the "hand shaker" to each and every person on Sunday morning. This writer has yet to find "hand shakes" as the prerequisite for entering the ministry, aside of course, from the "right hand of fellowship"!

of the sacraments?

The next time you speak about church to someone, try thinking about how you "advertise" your church to that person. You can instantly tell where your mind is at from the kind of advertising you want to put together. You can instantly tell how saturated by culture you have become, or maybe not become, by the way you think about what our church represents. How do you think about worshipping the Father? Is your thinking right? Do you seek happiness as a result of worship, or do you seek the righteousness of God in truth?

"Question 158: By whom is the word of God to be preached?
Answer 158: The word of God is to be preached only by such as
are sufficiently gifted, and also duly approved and called to that
office."

- Westminster Larger Catechism

"The ministry of the word was ordained for the planting and
watering of the church. The primary use, therefore, of this holy
function is, as we have already observed, the channel of com-
munication from the Head to the several members of the body."

- Charles Bridges, The Christian Ministry

"Not with preaching; all are not *didactikoi* (apt to teach, 1 Timothy 3:2). Nor *elegkikoi* (able to exhort and to convince gain-
sayers, Titus 1:9); all are not gifted and duly qualified. Some
are expressly prohibited from "Speaking in the Church" (1 Corinthians 14:34-35; 1 Timothy 2:12; Revelation 2:20) and none
other are to "preach unless they be sent" (Romans 10:15), nor to
"take such honor unto themselves unless they are called, etc."
(Hebrews 5:4-5). Are all and every one of the multitude of the
faithful able to teach, exhort and convince? Are they all sent to
preach? Are they all called of God, etc.? No, has not Christ laid
this task of Authoritative Preaching only upon His own officers
(Matthew 28:18-20)?"

- London Ministers of the Westminster Assembly,
Jus Divinum Regiminis Ecclesiastici:
The Divine Right of Church Government

☙ 5 ☙
Reformation of Evangelism

Matthew 28:16-20, "Then the eleven disciples went away into Galilee, to the mountain which Jesus had appointed for them. 17 When they saw Him, they worshiped Him; but some doubted. 18 And Jesus came and spoke to them, saying, "All authority has been given to Me in heaven and on earth. 19 "Go therefore and make disciples of all the nations, baptizing them in the name of the Father and of the Son and of the Holy Spirit, 20 "teaching them to observe all things that I have commanded you; and lo, I am with you always, even to the end of the age." Amen."

True Biblical Reformation must include the reformation of evangelism. The church growth movement today *markets* itself. It *does not evangelize*. The church this writer pastors is a small body of God's chosen people. It would not be difficult to "enlarge our borders" by tapping into marketing schemes that draw in unchurched Harry and Sally. Certainly, the church would grow rapidly if it was operating like a corporation. But Christ is not looking for a corporation, but an organically unified body sustained by the Head. He is looking for a remnant that is called out from among the world, not a corporate board that is copying the tactics of the world. Evangelism, then, in the

contemporary church is not only far off kilter, but is grossly ignorant of Christ's method for church growth. What the contemporary church believes is evangelism today must be thoroughly reformed if it is going to be pleasing to Christ. There is
no better passage of Scripture that directs the church than in
Matthew 28.

Matthew 28:16-20 demonstrates Christ's commission to authorize His *apostles* to *preach* the Gospel. The setting is quite
well-known. It is post-Resurrection. Actually, the realities behind the resurrection of Christ come to fruition practically in
this command to go out and disciple the nations. From the sur-
real feeling the disciples must have had seeing the truth of the
resurrection, to the hands-on commission, the resurrection
takes on shape and practical purpose in the lives of the disciples. Here the resurrection comes to its climax as Christ appears to His disciples and He will authorize His disciples to go
forth in His name and under His power. They receive here the
commission which has become the hallmark of this Gospel in
general, and probably one of its most beloved verses. It is not
simply the appearance of Jesus that caps the Gospel's message
here, but the words of Jesus to His disciples. What will the
remnant receive by way of instruction to further the work that
Christ constituted, and by what authority will they set out to
accomplish it?

The disciples return to Galilee as stated in verse sixteen,
"Then the eleven disciples went away into Galilee, to the mountain which Jesus had appointed for them." Not the twelve, but
the eleven disciples. Judas had started his journey to his own
place (eternal hell) as the *son of perdition* (John 17:12). From
that point forward the Gospel writers and the Luke/Acts narratives make it a point to clearly state that Judas is remembered
as a wicked, evil man. The disciples, on the other hand, had
been instructed to meet Jesus in Galilee and by a mountain He

designated. It is interesting that Jesus took care to choose a mountain close by the disciples, where they lived and where they certainly knew their home town. It has been traditionally seen as where the transfiguration took place.

In verse 17, the disciples see the risen Jesus, "When they saw Him, they worshiped Him; but some doubted." Upon seeing Jesus they worshipped Him, just as the women did upon seeing Him risen upon the Lord's Day morning. What other response would men take when seeing the risen Christ? Worship is due to the King of kings, and the disciples worshipped Him. This is the proper response of any subject of the King of Glory. Christ is not a resuscitated King, but a *resurrected* King. Here the disciples demonstrate their practical adoration of the stamp of approval on the work of the Mediator (the resurrection). They give homage to their Lord and God.

The text, though, adds a commentary on the attitude of some of them. It says that "some doubted." The Greek word here does not mean *unbelief*, nor does it mean *perplexity*. It has another meaning. It occurs in this verse and in Matthew 14:31 where Peter walks on the water but then becomes afraid. In Peter's case the idea surrounded being double minded. He had his eyes on the water and waves and the wind, *and* Jesus. Thus, Peter became fearful and began to sink. In the text at hand, this word points to the idea that there was uncertainty as to next steps. They doubted as to their mission. They doubted as to purpose. They were uncertain as to what Christ wanted them to do since they knew He was leaving and that some great transition from having His presence to not having His physical presence was taking place. The situation was "overwhelming" for them because all this was too much too fast. It would be inconsistent to think that first they all worshipped Him, which is exactly what the text states, and then some doubted as to whether it was really Jesus, or whether he was really alive, etc.

But it remains perfectly clear that *all* worshipped him and then *some* were uncertain, or needed some reassurance as to what the Risen Savior wanted from them next. "What do we do Jesus?" is the idea that some doubted as to how they should continue on.

In order to clear up any misconceptions or doubts as to "what's next," Jesus commissions them in verses 18-19. This section is actually subdivided into sections set in the context of Greek imperatives. Jesus tells them to "Go, make, baptize, and teach." These are all present participles that begin and continue. The participles when linked with the imperative verb take on imperatival force and function *as* imperatives. First, though, Christ gives a statement of His authority (verse 18b). "And Jesus came and spoke to them, saying, "All authority has been given to Me in heaven and on earth." Jesus was first *seen* by them, now He *comes* to them and *speaks* to them. He is not distant.

There is, first, an assertion of His authority. Christ, as Mediator, has fulfilled all that the Father had given Him to do, and does not *take* authority (although He would be perfectly right to take or dispose of any authority as God) but instead demonstrates that all authority had been *given* Him. Here is the universal dominion of the Covenant Mediator, the Elect Servant, who, by the authority of the Father makes a covenantal declaration. He has "ALL authority." All things are subject to Him. The wind and waves, even of a great hurricane, is no match for the all encompassing power of the Risen Christ. In fact He has all authority over Heaven and Earth. In other words, there is nothing in creation outside of His sovereign power and authority as King. This is commonly called the Office of Christ's Kingship. *The Westminster Larger Catechism* teaches that "Christ executeth the office of a king, in calling out of the world a people to himself, and giving them officers, laws, and censures, by which he visibly governs them; in bestowing saving grace upon his elect, rewarding their obedience, and correcting them for their sins, preserving and supporting them under all their temptations and sufferings, restraining and overcoming all their enemies, and powerfully ordering all things for his own glory, and their good; and also in taking vengeance on the rest, who know not God, and obey not the gospel." This is a summary of the authority Christ has as King over all of creation in association with the redemptive purposes that stand behind His work, death, resurrection and present intercession on behalf of His people.

Next, there is the command to make disciples of the nations in verse 19a. "Go therefore and make disciples of all the nations," The disciples are not allowed to sit back and wait for disciples to come to them. They are commanded to "go." The book of Acts demonstrates the hearty missionary endeavor of the church beginning in Jerusalem and extending into the utter parts of the earth. The disciples follow Christ's command. They "go" and "make" disciples. After the resurrection of Christ, the restriction of the Gospel message (the same Gospel that Abraham had) is now unleashed on all the nations and the disciples have a responsibility before their King to be pro-active for the Kingdom of God. These other nations had been in darkness. As a point of fact, God had caused them to walk in darkness, but now He has unleashed the Gospel freely and without restriction.

Jesus instructs the disciples (His chosen apostles) to make disciples. In the history of Salvation making disciples now reaches past the inclusivistic Jewish Nation, but also encompasses the outward inclusion of the Gentile nations. How Christ had long desired to gather the children of Jerusalem in, yet now, they are commanded by the Covenant Mediator to include the Gentiles, in fact, all nations. Discipleship to all nations is a

priority in the mind of Christ and how the Church is to function. But the church often mistakes discipleship for some sort
of rudimentary Sunday School class. This is not what Christ
has in mind. Making disciples has particular steps and relations.

It is important to note that Jesus introduces nothing new or
novel in this commissioning of His church officers, the eleven
apostles. Converts into Judaism had to go through vigorous
indoctrinations and ceremonial ritual in order to be part of the
Theocracy, which included the whole family being baptized.[1]
Discipleship is certainly something the Apostles knew about,
but now there is a more specific formula – the *Trinitarian*
Formula.

In verse 19b Jesus instructs them that they are to "Baptize
them", "baptizing them into the name of the Father and of the
Son and of the Holy Spirit." Baptism is not a new concept for
these men, and Jesus is not teaching something radically new.
Otherwise, no one would have every come out to the baptism of
John in the Judean wilderness, and the disciples would have
had a funny look on their faces saying "Baptism? What's that?"
The Old Testament is saturated with texts about the sprinkling
of the nations. Remember, the Old Testament was the Bible of
the disciples, and Jesus Christ. In Isaiah 44:3 the text says,
"For I will pour water on him who is thirsty, And floods on the
dry ground; I will pour My Spirit on your descendants, And My
blessing on your offspring." In Ezekiel 36:25 it says, "Then I
will sprinkle clean water on you, and you shall be clean; I will
cleanse you from all your filthiness and from all your idols."
Again, Isaiah 52:15 states, "So shall He sprinkle many nations."
Yet it is not simply the idea of sprinkling that Jesus initiates
here, but Baptism administered in the Trinitarian Formula, and

---

[1] This is much like the household baptisms throughout the book of Acts
which demonstrates the incorporation of Gentile converts to the faith.

yet into the single name of God. The disciples are now baptizing into the one name of God, not the many "names" of God. Here we find the disciples now baptizing in the *name* of the Father, Son and Spirit – the singular name of God.

Jesus is also inaugurating the covenant formula, a covenant relationship with the Mediator who subdues His converts by two things, Word and Sacrament. A sacrament is a visible sign of the Word. *The Westminster Confession of Faith* says, "A sacrament is a holy ordinance instituted by Christ, wherein, by sensible signs, Christ, and the benefits of the new covenant, are represented, sealed, and applied to believers." They are sprinkled by baptism and the sign of the covenant is placed upon them. *The Westminster Larger Catechism* states in Question 165, "Baptism is a sacrament of the New Testament, wherein Christ hath ordained the washing with water in the name of the Father, and of the Son, and of the Holy Ghost, to be a sign and seal of ingrafting into himself, of remission of sins by his blood, and regeneration by his Spirit; of adoption, and resurrection unto everlasting life; and whereby the parties baptized are solemnly admitted into the visible church, and enter into an open and professed engagement to be wholly and only the Lord's." This is the shift that is taking place – baptism is no longer done in the name of God, but in the name of God expressed as *Trinity*. It is the consummation of the authority of the Messianic King that is in view. It is applied in this manner to arrest covenant members to responsible covenant participation.

Not only are the disciples to "go, and "make" and "baptize", but they are also to "teach." Verse 20a says, "teaching them", "teaching them to observe all things that I have commanded you." Though all the Gospels are filled with historical narrative and teaching, Matthew's Gospel is particular to this idea of "teaching" housed through his Gospel in several sections of "teachings". This is especially seen in the Sermon on the Mount in Matthew 5-7. Those enrolled in Christ's Church must be taught. They are not taught then enrolled, but the disciples go, make disciples of all nations by baptizing, and *then* they teach them.

It is important to note that Christ is speaking to the eleven. This is not a blanket statement for the church. This is for the eleven – the officers in the church - to teach the Word and to administer the Sacraments. They are to teach "everything" Christ commanded them. Teaching is a function of the office that is set with administering the sacraments. It is an exceedingly tall order to teach everything Christ taught and this is not left up to the whim and fancy of every member of the church. Christ knew the Old Testament comprehensively. He took the Old Testament and commentated on it and expanded the disciple's understanding of key ideas and key truths bringing all the teaching into one comprehensive salvation history culminating in His work – His life, death, resurrection and present intercession. They are bound to teach everything He commanded them to teach, and that is coupled with the command to administer the sacraments to His church, those called out of every nation.

In this great teaching, there is a great promise – He will be with His disciples. The promise of Jesus' presence is found in verse 20b, "and lo, I am with you always, even to the end of the age." Amen." It is a forceful statement, and it applies to the commission itself, and based on the *magnitude* of the commission. Thus we see a common reoccurrence in the manner Matthew relays this information: all authority, all nations, all are baptized and all are taught. But "all this" can only be accomplished by Christ's Mediatorship, through the sent Spirit. It is certainly not that the Spirit was not in the Old Testament saint, or was not with the Old Testament saint, but here, as Christ is seated as the resurrected Mediator and King of the New Covenant, the Spirit is directly administered and sent by Him and the Father to draw and convert the elect, and to aid and equip the church for its continued and expanded task. The resurrected Redeemer had never sent the Spirit before. There was no Resurrected Redeemer until now. Certainly the Father and Son had sent the Spirit, since the Father and Son *always* send the Spirit. Yet, the Spirit had never been sent by the Resurrected Redeemer, the Son who took upon Himself human flesh, lived, died, and was raised to life. His redemptive work necessitates a "new way" of "sending" the Spirit, and as Christ said, He would not leave the apostles without a Comforter after His ascension to heaven. As the Gospel begins with "Emmanuel, God with us" so it ends with "Lo I am with you always." It is only through the presence of Christ that the task of the Church is accomplished. Jesus declares His authority, commissions His officers, and assures them of His continued presence in the future for ministry.

What the Text Teaches Us About the Great Commission

Here is a primary point to gather from this crucial text: the Great Commission, as intended by Jesus Christ, was given to His officers and surrounds the teaching of the Word, and the Administration of the Sacraments. Many Christians often take this statement "Go, make, baptize and teach" as a blanket statement for each and every individual Christian; from little 10 year old Johnny in the Metropolitan Sunday School class, to Grandma Jones in the backwoods of the Blue Ridge Mountains. However, this discourse by Christ was, 1) given to the eleven officers of His church, and 2) surrounds the administration of the Word and the administration of the Sacraments in making converts to the visible Church. Is this a great commission? Assuredly. But is this a great commission to all Christians in the same way? Not remotely. That is why a thorough and full understanding of Biblical Evangelism is so key in accomplishing *Christ's* work of building *Christ's* Church in the manner that *Christ* desired.

It is not that those who are not officers in the church are not engaged in evangelism – quite the contrary (and it is important to note this). Yet, it is exceedingly important to go about building the church in the manner that Christ dictates regardless of pragmatism (which teaches that the ends justify the means). Christians are no doubt commanded to be engaged in being witnesses in the world. But this is not the great commission found in Matthew 28.

The ministry of the Church surrounds only two means by which Christ will build His church (Matthew is very keen on this throughout his Gospel). The first is the Ministry of the Word, and the second is the Ministry of the Sacraments. The promise of Christ's continued presence and blessing, "Lo I am with you always" is contingent upon the manner in which His desires are followed. The promise of blessing only applies to these two means of grace that Christ instituted as a commission for His disciples. It does not apply to "slick marketing schemes" that draw in thousands of people, or "ad campaigns that brand a church in a given demographic."

Contemporary Marketing for the contemporary church is like a "Sampler Appetizer" at a restaurant – it presses those who come into contact with such a sampler to ask, "Who has the best assortment and sampler for me and my family?" They will then ask questions like: Does the Church have a youth group? Does it have a men's ministry or women's ministry? Does it have am evangelistic paint by numbers class? Does it have something for singles? What outreach group has it formulated? Does it promote activities like Beachfest? For them, face painting and the Gospel make a good combination. But it comes down to thinking through "What is the best way that we can lure Harry and Sally into the church?" These are the questions of *modern* evangelism and missions. This is what 21st Century Christendom believes will grow churches, and they are right - they will grow churches. But that is not what God is after. God is after worshippers of the Father who worship in Spirit and Truth and are taught rightly by the officers of His church who hold to the convictions of teaching that truth to the people of God.

Christian Books are published that outline both simple and complex marketing steps to growing a church. Rick Warren's biblically inaccurate book, "The Purpose Driven Church" outlines how you can take your small cell group to mega church status by copying the same principles that CEOs use to develop successful corporations. Why is Warren's book so popular? It is so popular because it uses "christinaese" (language that reflects biblical phrases and terminology), so it seems Christian enough, and it actually does grow churches. If anyone charismatic enough utilizes the business mogul mentality for their church, they will find that it really works. And, it will bring in revenue because more parishioners means more tithes. Theologically, it also demonstrates that the heretical Arminian man-centered appealing message of a different Gospel resonates loudly with unchurched Harry and Sally. Thus, if one changes the mode, and the message, to follow worldly standards and ideas, and makes them suitable to the audience, results will follow. This is, to use a biblical term, an "abomination" in the eyes of God, and an affront to Christ's biblical method of evangelism.

Jesus' plan of action is much simpler, and is comprised in four verses. The only means that Christ has promised to 1) be with the Church in, and 2) constitute the growth of the church is by the Word and Sacraments. There is no other means that

Christ will dwell in the midst of His people. There is no other means by which he will bring in and gather His elect from the world. Other ministries and other outreach tactics simply detract from the glory of God's ordained means of evangelism. God has not promised to bless face painting, parades and puppet shows, or the methodology of corporate America. Instead, He promises to *spiritually* bless the true preaching of His Word, and the right administration of the sacraments.

What determines effectiveness in outreach ministry? What determines effectiveness in evangelism? Another way of asking this same question by a rhetorical answer is to ask, "What is God's ordained means toward building His church?"

The ministry of the Word is God's primary means of His self-revelation to His creatures. *The Westminster Larger Catechism* question 158 states, "By whom is the word of God to be preached?" It answers, "The word of God is to be preached only by such as are sufficiently gifted, and also duly approved and called to that office." Thus, rightly, ministers of the Gospel, those appointed to administer the word and sacraments, are to be approved and called to that office. Jeremiah 14:15 demonstrates that those heralding God's word are sent by God, "Therefore thus says the LORD concerning the prophets who prophesy in My name, whom I did not send, and who say, 'Sword and famine shall not be in this land' - 'By sword and famine those prophets shall be consumed!" In Ephesians 4:8-13 Paul writes, "Therefore He says: "When He ascended on high, He led captivity captive, and gave gifts to men." (Now this, "He ascended" what does it mean but that He also first descended into the lower parts of the earth? He who descended is also the One who ascended far above all the heavens, that He might fill all things.) And He Himself gave some to be apostles, some prophets, some evangelists, and some pastors and teachers, for the equipping of the saints for the work of ministry, for the edi-

fying of the body of Christ, till we all come to the unity of the
faith and of the knowledge of the Son of God, to a perfect man,
to the measure of the stature of the fullness of Christ." These
are men Christ gave to the church, not those who appoint
themselves to offices they want to be in. The Resurrected Christ gifts men for pastoring, for preaching, so that they can subsequently build disciples in the work of their ministry. Malachi
2:7 states that these messengers of God should be trained men,
"For the lips of a priest should keep knowledge, and people
should seek the law from his mouth; for he is the messenger of
the LORD of hosts." And Paul boasts in God when he says in 2
Corinthians 3:6, that God "also made us sufficient as ministers
of the new covenant." God is the only one who can make a minister of the Gospel. And not all people in the church are ministers of the Gospel. If they were all ministers, then there would
be no one to minister the Word to, and the church itself would
be practically overthrown by a theory of "equality." In the
Form of Presbyterian Church Government, the Westminster
Assembly summarizes this point when they said, "The officers
which Christ hath appointed for the edification of his church,
and the perfecting of the saints, are, some extraordinary, as
apostles, evangelists, and prophets, which are ceased. Others
ordinary and perpetual, as pastors, teachers, and other church-
governors, and deacons."

The Sacraments are another form of the ministered Word
visibly. Sacraments are given by ministers of the Word for the
entrance into the church (in which in Matthew 16 and 18 the
keys or authority were given to the Apostles to allow or forbid
entrance by church discipline) and building up of the body.
Baptism ushers them in, and then they are to be taught, and
they are to subsequently grow. Baptism is noted by birth –
which is entrance into the church. The Sacrament of the Lord's
Supper is noted by conscious growth – which is signified by

nourishment. Everyone is not authorized to teach and administer the sacraments. One might say, "Are you saying that Christ appointed only 11 men to teach the Word and Administer the Sacraments?" That is exactly what the *text* says. It must be noted that the narrative does not speak about the women who saw Him on resurrection morning, or the 500 He appeared to. The book of Acts demonstrates, though, the continued reception and propagation of this commission through the eleven apostles to other elders who were later made disciples and then sent out in an official capacity to preach the Word. Phillip was a prototype deacon and evangelist. Stephen was a prototype deacon. Apollos, after being instructed more readily, was sent out as a "minister" according to 1 Corinthians 3:5, and may have even written the book of Hebrews. Timothy and Titus were both elders who were ordained by the laying on of hands by the eldership to pastor their respective churches. Epaphras, in Colossians 1:7, is said to be a fellow "*diakonia*" (servant) and minister. Ministers were set in office by specific methods and for official purposes.

Does this ministry of the Word and Sacrament by ministers detract from believers in their personal evangelism? Not at all. The Christian's daily exercise and witness of his faith pervades every area of life. They are living testimonies to the Word and Sacraments. The world is a dark blanket of sin and each Christian is a light that is created and sustained by the Word and Sacraments. Individually they light a house – as Christ says – and collectively, they are like a city on a hill (Matthew 5:14ff). 1 Peter 3:15-16 says, "But sanctify the Lord God in your hearts, and always be ready to give a defense to everyone who asks you a reason for the hope that is in you, with meekness and fear; having a good conscience, that when they defame you as evildoers, those who revile your good conduct in Christ may be ashamed." Peter encourages the church to be able to give an answer, or a defense of what people see. People cannot read minds. Thus must see something. People ask about what they see, what strikes them as different. In the Christian, they should see the hope that lies in them because Christians are not partaking of their evil deeds and rather, standing as a good witness against them. What then is the Christian to do?

Christians should be proactively engaged in bringing people to Christ. One of the most effective ways that this can occur is to invite people to church. Invite them to sit under the preaching of the Word and the administration of the Sacraments. Place them under the conduit means of grace that God has instituted for the conversion of souls. God will bless the efforts of the Christian in giving an answer to the hope that lies in them when people ask why they are so different, and subsequently use those opportunities to bring people (draw them) under the means of grace. It is not that every Christian is to stand up on the corner with their bibles and become iterant preachers. But instead, in every area of life, in every vocation, in every sphere, they are to affect, what the Gospel of Matthew says in Christ's teaching, preservation (salt and its saltiness) by outward witness, and yes, sometimes vocal witness against evil. They are, as disciples, witnesses to the changed reality that is affected by the High Priest through the Spirit, through preaching and administration of the sacraments, and demonstrate the converting power of Christ in their own life. There, they are ready to give an answer for the hope that lies in them. In opposition to this the 21st century Contemporary Church gains marketed converts. But Christ told his eleven ministers to make disciples.

How the Great Commission Applies to True Reformation

Reforming Evangelism is paramount to church growth and calling in the elect from all over the world as Christ insists.

What is the motivating factor for mission in general in most churches? Ask yourself, "What is my motivation for evangelism and missions?" Do you even have a motivation? Is it that you simply want warm bodies in church? The Methodist Church down the street from this writer's church has a sign that says "Come and use our stove to cook your food." This is very slick and clever. Harmless. Yes, very harmless. Evangelism? *They* think so. Instead, why is it that we can never find a sign that says, "Come and hear us preach to you about your sin and misery and the remedy found in Jesus Christ who is the only way to heaven." Would anyone come? Does it matter if some would come or not if the message that Christ wanted us to preach was true? Should we change the method and message to accommodate book sales and church grow? Really, based on Christ's explicit directives for ministry to the first eleven officers in His church, He was profoundly clear about how church growth works. Disciples are made by preaching and teaching the Word. Disciples are made by baptizing and administering the means of grace found in the sacraments. That is why the Apostles saw this as such an important duty that in Acts 6 they could not be weighed down with doing anything other than administering the Word and praying for power. That is why we have deacons to take up the responsibilities that must be done, but are not as important than the ministry of the Word of God in preaching and administering the Sacraments.

If our churches want to be successful in evangelism, our respective roles in that evangelistic endeavor first must be defined, and then must be enacted. What is Christ saying to the eleven disciples? In the most basic terms, He is directing them to bring back into covenant relations, covenant members who are already covenant breakers in Adam. It is utterly impossible for us to do any evangelistic work without understanding Christ's covenantal exhortation to the disciples. Make disciples, make covenant members by initiating sacraments and teaching them everything that Christ has taught the disciples about being in Covenant Relations with the Father. Is not that what the Father is seeking? How do we engage this structured simple approach? To be a missionary in its most basic term, really, is to stand for Christ in our vocations and in all our activities that have been ordained for us as good works that we walk in as covenant members in His Church. Whether we are mothers, or wives, or house cleaners, or hair dressers, or media consultants, or managers, to be involved in the mission of the church is to outwardly demonstrate the converting power of Christ in such a way that prompts questions about what it means to be a disciple, a covenant worshipper of the Father. People will come to you to get answers if you are truly acting like a Christian. The Christian's outward witness is key to church growth. The ministry of the Word and the ministry of the Sacraments should have such a profound affect on you and in you that it overflows into your outward daily life, with all your contacts and with all your personal interactions. (Hold that thought for a moment.)

The work of evangelism for the Reformed Church has never changed. October 31st is what we celebrate as *Reformation Day*. On that day we commemorate Christian Evangelism. The epicenter and height of biblical Christian Evangelism can be seen in two places in history – the era of Christ and His Apostles, and the time of the Great Reformation. The Reformation brought back to light the work of the Resurrected and glorified Christ through the Church's ministry of Word and Sacraments. In our current day, the Contemporary 21st century Church redefines Word and Sacrament and tries to dress them up to become attractive ploys to gain converts. That what the Roman Catholic Church did. That is why the Reformation worked so well against such a ploy – it simply instituted what Christ said was His ordained means of salvation and growth. If that is grasped, then that is really a redefining of the mission of the Church.

Jesus told the disciples to go, and the Contemporary church tells people to come. "Look at what we have to offer." Evangelism becomes marketing in that way. The Roman Church did the very same thing against the Reformers and Protestant church, just in a different way. They took the Word and Sacraments used them as a tool for power and manipulation. The Contemporary 21st Century Church uses them as manipulation too – they dress it up to attract people. The Reformers' radical turn from the Roman Catholic Church on this point was to preach the Law and the Gospel about what power there was in the Resurrected Christ and His present intercession, and then to reapply the present ministry of the priesthood of all believers in their respective roles in the church to further propagate the glory of God in the world. In the year 1517 it was radical to preach about Covenant Relationships by the grace of God. The only "relationship" that 13th-16th century parishioners knew was the power of authority, not in Christ, but in the Roman Church that abused authority. It went from Christ's Commission to make disciples, to Rome's commission to make superstitious people dependent on the Pope. That is why the reformation was so powerful in its evangelism – they started to preach the Word again, and brought people back into a covenant relationship with God through the Word and Sacraments. That was their primary aim.

What do people need most? People need the preaching the Word and administration of the sacraments most because that is where God and Christ are found. Take that which the people need most, corrupt it, and you corrupt the church. Give it back, and the church experiences the greatest revival in the History of the Church since the time of the Apostles. It was never a question as it the manner of marketing – for the Reformation it was the motto "back to the sources." The Reformers brought people back to the Bible, and the officers of Christ's church went back to studying Hebrew and Greek. It is no mistake, then, that revival began in the Reformation *with the officers in Christ's church.* It was Martin Luther, John Calvin, Ulrich Zwingli, William Tyndale, John Wycliffe – pastors and theologians – who were used to spark revival in the midst of those churning centuries. The Church of Rome would not even allow the people to partake of the complete Supper! But the Reformers followed Christ's simple commands to minister by Word and Sacraments as outlined in Matthew 28.

What did the Reformers do that any church in the world cannot do? Nothing! The entire life of the church revolved around the Word and Sacraments as Christ instituted them through the officers in the church, and ministered to the people. However, if pastors do not accomplish their job in rightly dividing the Word of truth for their people, then the people's job can never take place as faithful witnesses in their daily practice. That Word cannot go anywhere if it is not first rightly given. On that note alone, do you see what a mess the contemporary church is in evangelistically when the Word is not fully and truly preached? The church today thinks it is more effective if they couple a watered down Gospel (which is no Gospel at all) with drawing people in by face painting and parades. Instead, those who rightly preach will create a biblically educated laity. They in turn will be living witnesses to the power of Christ's High Priestly intercession through the Word and Sacraments. That in turn sparks conversations so that they can invite people to church to sit under the Word and Sacraments. Evangelism, then, has some specific stages. It draws people in by seeing how good of a Christian people in a given church should be (and that should spark you to consider your walk and demeanor). Your evangelistic encounters are a very good way testing how the Word of God is actually affecting you, or not. And then it sets those people that come into contact with you, by your godly direction, under the officers in the church who, by extension, are going, making, baptizing and teaching disciples all that Christ commanded. Pastors, then, must be examining themselves to be sure 1) they are ministering by way of Word and Sacraments, and 2) that their respective congregations are being affected and becoming living testimonies to Christ' blessed work. Only then will others see that light and be drawn in by the Father. This is the only way that evangelism will ever become reformed.

"Besides the publick worship in congregations, mercifully established in this land in great purity, it is expedient and necessary that secret worship of each person alone, and private worship of families, be pressed and set up; that, with national reformation, the profession and power of godliness, both personal and domestick, be advanced."

- Westminster Directory for Family Worship

"Family Worship, as the name imports, is the joint worship rendered to God, by all the members of one household."

- J.W. Alexander, Family Worship

❧ 6 ❧

Reformation of the Family

Joshua 24:15, "And if it seems evil to you to serve the LORD, choose for yourselves this day whom you will serve, whether the gods which your fathers served that were on the other side of the River, or the gods of the Amorites, in whose land you dwell. But as for me and my house, we will serve the LORD."

The reformation of the family unit is God's primary ordained setting of teaching and instructing His people. In an age where the family is under attack, the topic of the family must come to the forefront. Statistics can be somewhat "relative" but here are a few that should spark the church to take "family life" more seriously, and pattern it after God's model. In the course of a year in America, according to the census bureau, almost one million husbands beat their wives regularly. 25% of American wives report being molested or raped by their husband. Ten million children are violently abused by their parents. (50% of those men who abuse their wives abuse their children.) 17.8% of teenage girls are sexually abused by their boyfriends. One out of eight of these teenage girls that become pregnant are further abused by the father of their baby. Millions of children are currently being raised by single or divorced parents, guardians, parents of different religions or races, gay or lesbian parents, and adoptive parents. Single parents account for 27% percent of family households with children under 18. One in two children will live in a single-parent family at some point in childhood. One in three children is born to unmarried parents. Between 1978 and 1996, the number of babies born to unmarried women per year quadrupled from 500,000 to more than two million. The number of single mothers increased from three million to 10 million between 1970 and 2000. Nearly half of all marriages end in divorce. More than one million children have parents who separate or divorce each year. More than half of Americans today have been, are or will be in one or more stepfamily situations. One child out of 25 lives with neither parent. An estimated 550,000 children were in foster care as of March 31, 1999, a 35% increase since 1990. About 120,000 of these children were waiting for permanent adoptive families. In 1993 (the last year national statistics are available), kinship providers cared for about a third of the foster children in New York, 40 percent of foster children in California and nearly half of foster children in Illinois. [1] In 1999, adoptions were finalized for more than 17,000 foster children; another 18,000 children were living in foster homes, waiting for adoptions to be completed, and about 20,000 foster children were legally available for adoption but had not yet been placed in their new homes.[2] There has also been a massive surge in gay and lesbian headed/unmarried households. Between six million and 10 million children of lesbian, gay and bisexual parents currently live in the United States.[3] The number of unmarried partner households has increased by 72 percent in the last decade from three

---

[1] CRS Report for Congress: Foster Care and Adoption Statistics
[2] US Census Bureau Press Release
[3] American Bar Association, 1987, Children of Lesbians and Gays Everywhere (COLAGE)

million in 1990 to more than five million in 2000. These figures include both same-sex and different-sex couples.[4] One-third of lesbian households and one-fifth of gay male households have children.

There is no doubt that not only has the American family changed in the last 40 years, but it has changed for the worse. Instead of embracing the biblical norm for the reformation of the family, many Christians today are also part of these statistics (though certainly not all of them). If the church believes that the family is as important as God intended it, then changes must be made. In looking at the text of Joshua 24, there is much to glean there in response to the degradation and destruction of the family.

Joshua 24:1-28: Then Joshua gathered all the tribes of Israel to Shechem and called for the elders of Israel, for their heads, for their judges, and for their officers; and they presented themselves before God. 2 And Joshua said to all the people, "Thus says the LORD God of Israel: 'Your fathers, including Terah, the father of Abraham and the father of Nahor, dwelt on the other side of the River in old times; and they served other gods. 3 'Then I took your father Abraham from the other side of the River, led him throughout all the land of Canaan, and multiplied his descendants and gave him Isaac. 4 'To Isaac I gave Jacob and Esau. To Esau I gave the mountains of Seir to possess, but Jacob and his children went down to Egypt. 5 'Also I sent Moses and Aaron, and I plagued Egypt, according to what I did among them. Afterward I brought you out. 6 'Then I brought your fathers out of Egypt, and you came to the sea; and the Egyptians pursued your fathers with chariots and horsemen to the Red Sea. 7 'So they cried out to the LORD; and He put darkness between you and the Egyptians, brought the sea upon them, and covered them. And your eyes saw what I

---

[4] Council on Contemporary Families

did in Egypt. Then you dwelt in the wilderness a long time. 8 'And I brought you into the land of the Amorites, who dwelt on the other side of the Jordan, and they fought with you. But I gave them into your hand, that you might possess their land, and I destroyed them from before you. 9 'Then Balak the son of Zippor, king of Moab, arose to make war against Israel, and sent and called Balaam the son of Beor to curse you. 10 'But I would not listen to Balaam; therefore he continued to bless you. So I delivered you out of his hand. 11 'Then you went over the Jordan and came to Jericho. And the men of Jericho fought against you -- also the Amorites, the Perizzites, the Canaanites, the Hittites, the Girgashites, the Hivites, and the Jebusites. But I delivered them into your hand. 12 'I sent the hornet before you which drove them out from before you, also the two kings of the Amorites, but not with your sword or with your bow. 13 'I have given you a land for which you did not labor, and cities which you did not build, and you dwell in them; you eat of the vineyards and olive groves which you did not plant.' 14 " Now therefore, fear the LORD, serve Him in sincerity and in truth, and put away the gods which your fathers served on the other side of the River and in Egypt. Serve the LORD! 15 "And if it seems evil to you to serve the LORD, choose for yourselves this day whom you will serve, whether the gods which your fathers served that were on the other side of the River, or the gods of the Amorites, in whose land you dwell. But as for me and my house, we will serve the LORD." 16 So the people answered and said: "Far be it from us that we should forsake the LORD to serve other gods; 17 "for the LORD our God is He who brought us and our fathers up out of the land of Egypt, from the house of bondage, who did those great signs in our sight, and preserved us in all the way that we went and among all the people through whom we passed. 18 "And the LORD drove out from before us all the people, including the Amorites who dwelt in the land. We also will serve the LORD, for He is our God." [19] But Joshua said to the people, "You cannot serve the LORD, for He is a holy God. He is a jealous God; He will not forgive your transgressions nor your sins. [20] "If you forsake the LORD and serve foreign gods, then He will turn and do you harm and consume you, after He has done you good." [21] And the people said to Joshua, "No, but we will serve the LORD!" [22] So Joshua said to the people, "You are witnesses against yourselves that you have chosen the LORD for yourselves, to serve Him." And they said, "We are witnesses!" [23] "Now therefore," he said, "put away the foreign gods which are among you, and incline your heart to the LORD God of Israel." [24] And the people said to Joshua, "The LORD our God we will serve, and His voice we will obey!" [25] So Joshua made a covenant with the people that day, and made for them a statute and an ordinance in Shechem. [26] Then Joshua wrote these words in the Book of the Law of God. And he took a large stone, and set it up there under the oak that was by the sanctuary of the LORD. [27] And Joshua said to all the people, "Behold, this stone shall be a witness to us, for it has heard all the words of the LORD which He spoke to us. It shall therefore be a witness to you, lest you deny your God." [28] So Joshua let the people depart, each to his own inheritance.

The context of this chapter in Joshua is a theologically central chapter. Here Joshua addresses *all* the people, not simply the leaders of the tribes, or those who may be deemed the "important" people. At this time of covenant renewal, all of the people from all of the tribes are important. In chapter one of this book on reformation in dealing with Josiah, what Joshua will do in the context of this biblical passage is reminiscent of what Josiah will do later in Israel's history.

The setting here is surrounding Joshua's farewell speech, or what may be considered his last sermon. Previously, chapter 23 explained obedience to the book of the Law, but here Joshua is prompting obedience to that Law. Joshua is in Shechem, a covenantally important location surrounding the vows and altar of Jacob, prompting the Israelites to covenant renewal. The text states in Joshua 24:25, "So Joshua made a covenant with the people that day, and made for them a statute and an ordinance in Shechem." The manner in which Joshua leads up to this covenant renewal is by laying out the basic structure of "covenant."

First, there is the preamble introducing the king (cf. v.2); Joshua 24:2 says, "Thus says the LORD God of Israel..." The Lord is the King in which all the Israelites should follow and worship. Then, some antecedent history describing previous relationships between the two parties is discussed (cf. vv 2–13). Joshua shows that God dealt with the patriarchs and explains how and why. Joshua 24:2 says, "Your fathers..." Then, he speaks about basic stipulations governing future relationships with "this king" (cf. vv 14, 16, 18b, 21, 23, 24). The text states in Joshua 24:14, "Now therefore, fear the LORD, serve Him in sincerity and in truth, and put away the gods which your fathers served on the other side of the River and in Egypt. Serve the LORD!" Next, Joshua lays out the blessings and curses (cf. vv 19–20). Joshua 24:20 makes this clear, "If you forsake the LORD and serve foreign gods, then He will turn and do you harm and consume you, after He has done you good." Then, there is an invocation of the "gods" as witnesses (cf. vv 22, 27), but in this case it is turned to the people of God. Joshua 24:22 says, " And they said, "We are witnesses!" This structure is a typical setting and structure for "covenant."

There are a number of key elements Joshua uses to address the people in what is called their "Salvation History." It is a recounting of what God has previously done for the people. It is looking to past grace to think about what the future holds. Two central promises are seen to be fulfilled though the covenant is not fulfilled. These were the presence of God directing the patriarchs and the gift of having a large family as God promised the fathers. Also, Moses and Aaron are mentioned; Moses representing the Law and word of God, and Aaron representing the priesthood and sacrifice. Then, God's military victories are numbered, and Balaam's treachery and downfall are stated. In essence, the point of all this "recounting" is that man has really done nothing, and God has acted on behalf of Israel for Israel's blessings. Israel's entire identity is a result of divine decree and action *not* human power.

In Joshua 24:14, the test states, "Now therefore, fear the LORD, serve Him in sincerity and in truth, and put away the gods which your fathers served on the other side of the River and in Egypt. Serve the LORD!" This is not a command to enact partially. It is a command to enact completely. It has an interesting New Testament parallel in John 4:24 where Christ says that worshippers that the Father seeks worship God in "spirit and truth". In "truth or faithfulness" is much the same as "spirit and truth." It seems that the charge that Joshua lays against them (acting somewhat like a court attorney for God) is that Israel really has not served God in the way God desires, and has fallen short. Even in Egypt they followed other gods, but God still heard their cries (verse 7). But, there is a choice to be made in their next venture.

The Israelites are entering a land in which religious choices must be made. That is why Joshua 24:15 is such a key text to this chapter. Here is found an interesting dilemma. In the land of Canaan the Israelites are going to have all sorts of gods to choose from. One could choose to follow the god of thunder, of fertility, of the mountains, etc. One could go one way or the other, one choice over another and no choice would be irrelevant since all the choices were at some level dealing with a particular problem a person may be having. But to claim *one God*, an ultimate authority, and discard the rest as "false", would actually be seen as crazy in the Canaanite culture. Basically, Joshua recalls Israel's history, and then asks Israel to make a choice to follow God because of who God is and what He has done, and not to pay attention to idols. Joshua 24:15 states, "And if it seems evil to you to serve the LORD, choose for yourselves this day whom you will serve, whether the gods which your fathers served that were on the other side of the River, or the gods of the Amorites, in whose land you dwell." It may seem crazy, but it not crazy because of who God is and what He has done – remember, Joshua says, *that God is God alone*. Then the principle text to heed is given, "But as for me and my house, we will serve the LORD."

The statement of Joshua to serve the Lord is the high point of this chapter. It is a twofold demand for continued obedient discipleship, set in the context of the *family*. "Me" – Joshua assigns obedience first to himself, and then says "my house" where he makes the conscious decision for his house to follow God as well. He is the federal head of his household before God. He desires to serve the Lord. This means "to serve as a subject, or, to labor as a servant." It holds the idea that Joshua and his family will be serving God sacrificially.

Now, it is important to note that this covenant renewal began *individually*, and then grew into the expression by way of the family unit for family reformation. It started with Joshua, then moved to Joshua's family. It surrounds the family's commitment, lead by the head of the family to serve God. It surrounds covenanting with God as a family, unlike the heathen nations. It is by necessity that family reformation take place to serve God as God would be served. And, it is by a choice that such family reformation is set in place and set in motion.

What the Text is Teaching Us

What does it mean to serve God? Theologically, this is a simple question to answer. As noted, the Hebrew idea behind Joshua's statement is to serve as in the Levitical priesthood – to *serve by sacrifice or worship*. This word "serve" is used nine times in this one chapter of Joshua. Joshua is making a conscious decision to worship God, and not serve idols. The Israelites have to make that choice as well. Will they worship and bow down to idols as the Canaanites will? Will they worship God instead? Serving God encapsulates the idea that this is the highest form of religious worship that can be accomplished. For example, Exodus 7:16 says, "And you shall say to him, 'The LORD God of the Hebrews has sent me to you, saying, "Let My people go, that they may serve Me in the wilderness". And Deuteronomy 6:13 states, "You shall fear the LORD your God and serve Him, and shall take oaths in His name." In 1 Samuel 12:24 the text read, "Only fear the LORD, and serve Him in truth with all your heart; for consider what great things He has done for you." In Psalm 100:2 a very familiar verse is given, "Serve the LORD with gladness; Come before His presence with singing." Others are of like sort:

Matthew 4:10, "Then Jesus said to him, "Away with you, Satan! For it is written, 'You shall worship the LORD your God, and Him only you shall serve.'"

Colossians 3:24, "...knowing that from the Lord you will receive the reward of the inheritance; for you serve the Lord Christ."

Hebrews 9:14, "...how much more shall the blood of Christ, who through the eternal Spirit offered Himself without spot to God, cleanse your conscience from dead works to serve the living God?"

Simply stated, service *is* worship. Worship is done both privately, by the family, and publicly, by the corporate gather-

ing of families. Families are critically important in the econ-
omy of God's saving work. Joshua did not say "we as a nation"
or "all of us as individuals." Rather, Joshua spoke *covenantally*. As the *federal head* of his family, he first turned to his
own life, then to his responsibility in leading his family. In this
way, his family would be as sanctified or lead to serve and worship God only so far as Joshua was sanctified and serving and
worshipping God. He says, "As for me" – the federal head, and
"my house" those I lead. God designed the family to be the
foundational covenant unit in this way. Joshua laid the service
and worship of God first on himself then on his family and so
desired that all the families of the tribes would do so as well.
God has so set up the family that it remains as the catalyst to
change and reformation both in society and the church.

From the time that God placed Adam and Eve as a family
unit in the garden, and all Adam's family (or posterity) fell with
him, so God has continued to use the covenantal organization
of the family all through salvation history. It is incontestable
that God worked through families through Israel's salvation
history – Abraham, Isaac, Jacob, Joseph, Moses, Joshua, etc.
right up and into the coming of Christ – who is the fullness of
the promise and covenant God made with Abraham as Zacha-
rias and Mary tell us in Luke 1, and into the book of Acts that
demonstrates God working through families as whole households are ushered into the church through the covenant signs,
both by circumcision and household baptisms. God has never
and will never stop utilizing the foundational covenant unit in
His saving acts. The family sets the environment that gives opportunity to the continual teaching of the word, and for prayer
and supplication in serving God. Just think about the Ten
Commandments and who they are addressed to: *heads of the
family*. Exodus 20:9ff says, "Remember the Sabbath day, to
keep it holy. Six days you shall labor, and do all your work, but

the seventh day is a Sabbath to the LORD your God. On it *you shall not do any work, you, or your son, or your daughter, your male servant, or your female servant, or your livestock, or the sojourner who is within your gates.*" Who is the "you?" It is the head of the household. And then, neither shall any other servants do work, or children, or livestock, on the Sabbath day. In this way God reckons the family as a small Government or Theocracy. It has a given structure with husband, wife and children. It is governed like a little church, which is why elders are must first rule their homes well before they rule the church (1 Tim. 3 and Titus 1). If they are unable to get family worship accomplished in the home, they have no right in leading worship in the church. The family is also a little economic center. Here the head of the house trains the family to be responsible stewards of what God has given them. As the family serves God in its capacity of familial worship and service, all other organizations and societal structures will change if the family unit changes. If the family is destroyed, society will crumble. If the family is restored and serving God, society will prosper. Joshua says in essence, "If you want to prosper in the land God has given you, serve God and not idols. Covenant as a family with God, serve Him and you will be blessed."

Family Worship is biblically necessary to serve God. God is to be worshipped by all, which includes the family. Psalm 66:4 says, "All the earth shall worship You And sing praises to You." This includes the family. As a matter of fact, it is directed to the family in a subtle manner since all the earth is made up of family units. What is "family worship?" Family worship is the joint worship rendered to God by all the members of one household. Families have always worshipped God. Biblical examples abound: Genesis 18:19, "For I have known him, in order that he may command his children and his household after him, that they keep the way of the LORD, to do righteousness and justice, that the LORD may bring to Abraham what He has spoken to him." The religious care of the family can be seen in the righteousness of Job; Job 1:5, "So it was, when the days of feasting had run their course, that Job would send and sanctify them, and he would rise early in the morning and offer burnt offerings according to the number of them all. For Job said, "It may be that my sons have sinned and cursed God in their hearts." Thus Job did regularly." Joshua 24:15 is the key text to follow, "But as for me and my house, we will serve the LORD." Jesus had a familiar relationship with His disciples as one who had no place to lay His head, and yet taught the Scriptures to them everywhere they went. They had a relationship of the Master to servant, and as he said in Matthew 12:50, "For whoever does the will of My Father in heaven is My brother and sister and mother." In Acts 10:1-2 there is listed the devote nature of Cornelius and his house, "There was a certain man in Caesarea called Cornelius, a centurion of the band called the Italian band, a devout man, and one that feared God with all his house.." Lois and Eunice are mentioned in 2 Timothy 1:5 as a great influence on Timothy by applying the Scriptures that would mold him for the rest of his life, and ultimately save him. It is impossible to make the argument that the family unit should not worship if God expects worship from all. Service to God is not done once a week for an hour. Service to God, to use Job's description, was *continual*. And it is no wonder that God singles Job out as one who *fears* God (worships God) and *shuns* evil. This is the very thing Joshua tells the Israel to do – serve God and forsake idols.

Family worship will induce the reformation of the family. This is God's means whereby He will transform the character and disposition of those in the family. However, reformation must begin with a single person before it can affect the family. Joshua as the federal head, or God appointed representative of his family, was first affected by following and serving God. Only by his action to serve God can he, with any great solemnity, cause his family to joyfully serve God as well. It only takes one obedient individual to affect others in this way. But it must start with someone. One preserver, one salty person, will preserve and affect others in a godly manner.

Who should lead family worship? Not everyone, obviously, is a bible scholar. The Scriptures place the responsibility of family worship on the head of the family. The federal head of the family (the father or husband) should lead their families to godly reform. Unless for some reason the head of the household is an ungodly man, the federal head (who will be discussed in a later chapter) should lead the family in reformation. God has given the federal headship to the man, who is the head of the women and the instructor of the family.

There is no passage in scripture that says "If he can't teach then he should abdicate his duties to his wife, or to some other person." Observation shows that families which have no household worship are at a low degree in spiritual mindedness. It is the father's responsibility to lead his family before God, or as Joshua said he would do, "serve God." Families that perform religious worship in a cold manner, or in a lazy manner, are little affected by it and by any means of grace.

Think about the affect that family worship has on the family. Family worship has a direct and manifest tendency to make religion a matter of everyday interest. If family worship is a daily activity, then it is expected and becomes part of the family régime. The things of God should be the predominant influence in any Christian home, and this happens by way of family worship.

How the Text Applies to Our Everyday Lives

As in Joshua's day, no less in our day is the choice made to

follow God. In our own day there is as much distraction from
family worship and the things of God as in Joshua's day – even
more so with contemporary media. It is much easier to choose
to replace family worship with something carnal than it is to
enact a plan for family worship. It is easier to watch TV, or to
plug in a video than to sit around the dinner table and worship
God. Dinnertime can certainly be an opportune time. Historically it may even be "the" best time, or even the God appointed
time, to make for your family worship, such as the morning or
evening sacrifice given at the altar. However, prudence should
dictate the best time that your family comes together to be
taught God's Word and to pray. But you must make a choice as
well. Will you serve the gods of the land, or will you enact family worship and serve God in your own families? What things
rule or influence your home most right now? If you were to give
an account right now of your home, would God be pleased with
your piety and the piety of your household? What influences
have you allowed into the home, and what influences need to be
taken out of the home? Does your family have a regular and
stable feeling of coming together to pray, or worship, or service
to God? Would *your family* say that your house is well ordered? Imagine the Day of Judgment when the individuals of
the house are judged for their family religion – what will they
say of *you*?

We ought, heartily, to examine ourselves in light of the reality that God not only desires, but commands family worship
through these various saintly examples, and if we neglect such
worship, we are neglecting to follow what God has plainly revealed to us in His word concerning such. One might claim to
be part of a "Reformed Church," but the church functions as a
result of the piety and religious attitude of its members which is
made of individual families. If those families are negligent in
the things that God desires of them, what kind of affect will

those families have on the church, and what kind of piety will be seen by those outside the church? Is your family a model of a little government rightly enacted? A little church? A little economic center? What kind of impact will your family have on the church, on society or the world?

The reformation of the family is more than simply saying a prayer at mealtime. Worship is more than uttering a prayer before you eat spaghetti. Federal heads of their families must realize the great influence God has given them over their families. The affects of your personal piety, and your resolve for worship and service of God on the members of the house, on the children of house, are eternally beneficial. If your family is more influenced by a pessimistic attitude toward life than it is your religious piety, what is modeling them? What will their resolve be? If they are more influenced by video games, or television than religion, what greater influence do they have? If they are more influenced by sports or recreation that family worship, what is going to shape them? No doubt the popular phrase was made famous by the fictional Forest Gump – "Stupid is as stupid does." Yes, but, stupid does *by what they see you do.*

The question is posed by Joshua to us as families, "What will we do now?" Excuses about time and ability are sinful ways of shucking responsibility and sinning against Christ. Christ abhors your non-interest to your family. It is not "But as for me I will serve the Lord." It is that "me and my house" will serve the Lord. Christ desires families to be reformed by His word and it is as imperative as covenant families to serve Him now, as in the day of Joshua. Turning to distractions is sin. Distractions pull us away from God and hinder growth before Him.

Whether we are in the 21st century, or the 5th century, or the 31st century, service to Christ never changes. Even more so now that we have the completion of His work and the direct influence of His Spirit sent from the very throne of the exalted Messiah, how shall we as families throw away the means by which God will reform us and ready us for service to Him? So what should you do right now? Examine your family. If you want a reformed family, your family must be engaged in service to God. Yes, you may be tired from a long day, the children have been misbehaving, or work was atrocious, or the keeping of the house may have been particularly hard with extra work, and so it is very easy to blow of the most important part of the day. Let us just say it and get it over with once and for all – God made things difficult by allowing sin to enter the world. Fallen minds and bodies and religion do not mix. Okay, now that we have said it, we need to get over it and move on to serving God. This is where we must mortify the flesh and submit to the Spirit and follow His directives for us. Examine your faithfulness to Christ in this. Take the day and evaluate and examine how well you guard your family against the influences of Canaan. Unless of course, it seems evil to you.

"Our houses must be churches; with ourselves we must give up our houses to the Lord, to be to Him for a name and a people."

– Rev. Matthew Henry, Church in the House

"The great duty of every husband is to love his own wife. This is the foundation of all the rest; this must be mixed with all the rest; this is the epitome of the rest of his duty. Fix but this blessed habit in the heart, and it will teach a man, yea, it will enforce a man, to all the tenderness, honor, care, and kindness, that is required of him."

- Rev. Richard Steele, What are the duties of Husband and Wife Toward Each Other?

❧ 7 ❧
Duties of Husbands

Ephesians 5:22-33, "Wives, submit to your own husbands, as to the Lord. ²³ For the husband is head of the wife, as also Christ is head of the church; and He is the Savior of the body. ²⁴ Therefore, just as the church is subject to Christ, so let the wives be to their own husbands in everything. ²⁵ Husbands, love your wives, just as Christ also loved the church and gave Himself for her, ²⁶ that He might sanctify and cleanse her with the washing of water by the word, ²⁷ that He might present her to Himself a glorious church, not having spot or wrinkle or any such thing, but that she should be holy and without blemish. ²⁸ So husbands ought to love their own wives as their own bodies; he who loves his wife loves himself. ²⁹ For no one ever hated his own flesh, but nourishes and cherishes it, just as the Lord does the church. ³⁰ For we are members of His body, of His flesh and of His bones. ³¹ "For this reason a man shall leave his father and mother and be joined to his wife, and the two shall become one flesh." ³² This is a great mystery, but I speak concerning Christ and the church. ³³ Nevertheless let each one of you in particular so love his own wife as himself, and let the wife see that she respects her husband."

The context of this passage is set in the edification of the Body of Jesus Christ. Paul is admonishing the church at Ephesus to be filled with the Spirit, and being filled with the Spirit (cf. v. 18) exemplifies itself in various ways. It demonstrates itself in ministering in song to one another, or giving thanks to God, or even in submitting to one another before God demonstrating a humble authority. Christ ministers to His people through His body in various ways. An arm has a function, a leg has a function, and so do the eyes, ears, feet, and hands. So as the head controls the body, Christ controls the Church authoritatively through its various members and their ministry to one another on behalf of the Head.

From instruction on the church, Paul moves into the Christian family which is completed in 6:9. The contrast here is given between Christ and the Church, and how the family unit is ordered. The family unit made up of husband and wife, is set against the parallel of Christ and the Church. As Christ and the Church act in relations, so to a great extent the husband and wife relate. Marriage, then, is forever, and Scripturally seen as positive and wonderfully mimicking the relationship that the Lord of Glory has with His Church.

It is interesting to note how Paul begins this comparison by utilizing "subjection" as his motif. Wives are subject to their husbands, as the church is subject to Christ. The argument is posed as interlaced between husbands and wives and between Christ and the Church. How does Christ love the Church? Christ is the Federal Head of the Church (v. 23), and as the Head of the Church He is the representative on behalf of the Church before God. In this representation, Christ governs the Church. He governs all her actions in His providence. This government is by coercion not suggestion, and in all this He is executing the office of a king. As Jesus said, "All authority..." is His (Matthew 28:16-20)." In this government, He protects her from not only her enemies, but also herself. She is, in certain sinful manners, a danger to herself as much as the enemies that surround her desire to tear her apart. In both ways, Christ protects her to build her up. As 1 Corinthians 15:25 states, "For He must reign till He has put all enemies under His feet."

In this governing, Christ also preserves the Church. This means He gives her grace and spirit power   Isaiah 63:9 says, "In all their affliction He was afflicted, And the Angel of His Presence saved them; In His love and in His pity He redeemed them; And He bore them and carried them All the days of old." He also provides for the church when He nourishes her for her good and well being. Romans 8:28 says, "And we know that all things work together for good to those who love God, to those who are the called according to His purpose." All of this is done because Christ is the Savior of His Church and preserves and provides everything for her well being.

Paul makes mention of this (that Christ is the Savior of the Church) in verse 23. This is a demonstration of the office of Christ as the Savior of the body. *The Westminster Confession of Faith* states, "The Lord Jesus, by his perfect obedience, and sacrifice of himself, which he, through the eternal Spirit, once offered up unto God, hath fully satisfied the justice of his Father; and purchased, not only reconciliation, but an everlasting inheritance in the kingdom of heaven, for all those whom the Father hath given unto him."[1] This means that Christ has covenantally sought out the Church to redeem her by joining the Father and Spirit in the Covenant of Redemption to minister to the Church all the benefits and fruits of that covenant in the Covenant of Grace. In other words, He loved the Church in giving Himself up for the Church. He covenanted with the Father and Spirit to do this, and then ministered those benefits to His Church through the Covenant of Grace.

---

[1] *Westminster Confession of Faith* 8:5

Jesus Christ loves the Church as His body (cf. v. 30). Hebrews 2:17 says, "Therefore, in all things He had to be made like His brethren, that He might be a merciful and faithful High Priest in things pertaining to God, to make propitiation for the sins of the people." Romans 5:8 states, "But God demonstrates His own love toward us, in that while we were still sinners, Christ died for us." In this union Christ is organically joined to the church. John 6:53 says, "Then Jesus said to them, "Most assuredly, I say to you, unless you eat the flesh of the Son of Man and drink His blood, you have no life in you." He sanctifies the Church by the Word. He makes her holy and without blemish. Ephesians 5:26, "... that He might sanctify and cleanse her with the washing of water by the word..." In all of this, He demonstrates His work as the Federal Head of His people.

What does it mean that *Christ* is the Federal Head of His people? Yes, he is a representative, but there is much more than simply that notion. It is the construct of authority that God placed Christ in. How might a Christian understand this in a more simple fashion? Well, Paul makes this incredibly easy when he demonstrates the work of Christ as Federal Head is much like the union between the *husband* over the wife. The husband is the head of the wife, the representative before God on behalf of the family. The husband governs the family. This government is by coercion not suggestion. The family in this way is not a democracy. Instead, the husband is to mimic, in a godly manner, the authority parallel that Christ has over the Church. This is an imitation of Christ's Kingly government over the church. However, the king is never governing at the expense of His love. Paul is not setting up a tyrannical dictator over the family here. Rather, like Christ who died for His church, the husband dies daily for his wife. He does not come to be served, but to serve. He does this, though, in his authority over her and the family.

The husband, like Christ, should protect his family. This mimics Christ's Kingly protection over the church. The husband should also preserve his family, mimicking Christ's power to preserve through teaching the Word. The husband should be able to provide for his family, mimicking Christ's ability to provide both materially and spiritually. In this way, the husband is to love His wife as he loves his own body.

All other duties that the husband accomplishes on behalf of his wife are comprised in the love and great affection the husband is bound by duty to the wife. One must understand the difference between something that is done merely out of duty, and one that is done out of love/duty. One is done out of expressed obligation to the wife without necessary feeling anything (that is mere duty) and the love/duty is done from a heartfelt obligation to fulfill a duty to God on behalf of the wife who reaps the benefit of both the duty and the affection behind the duty. If a husband was to take his wife out to a fine meal, have a wonderful conversation with her, treat her "special" and then upon returning home the wife says, "Thanks for a lovely evening," what should be the husband's response? If he says, "It is my duty to do so," and leaves it at that, he can probably expect to sleep on the couch that night. Rather, the husband should deal tenderly with her as his heart is so moved to minister to her as her authoritative *head* that preserves, protects and provides for her. No duty to the wife could be accomplished without love, for all begrudging service is sin.

Paul brings this point home when he explains that he who does not love in his duty hates his wife. Why is this so? It is because the husband is joined to his wife. He is covenantally and organically joined to her. He is bound by covenant before God to her (Genesis 2:23-25). Marriage is not just a piece of paper handed in and signed at the courthouse. The husband is joined organically to her. This is why Paul's argument surrounds treating the wife as the husband's own body. This is where they become one flesh literally and spiritually.

What We Learn from the Text

The meaning of this text in full is quite plain to the Christian reader - the duties of the Federal Husband follow the analogy of Christ and the Church in that the husband is to love his wife as Christ loved the Church. For the husband it does not get any simpler than that, while at the same time the object of fulfillment remains daunting.

One of the first things to note about marriage in this respect is that God has providentially set the husband and wife together. God is the great matchmaker. He decrees, from the foundation of the world, who will marry who and when. To uphold the duty of the husband, a husband must first acknowledge that God has providentially given this woman to him. Think about Genesis 24:6-7, "Then Isaac brought her into his mother Sarah's tent; and he took Rebekah and she became his wife, and he loved her. So Isaac was comforted after his mother's death." In reading this whole narrative, one finds that God providentially set these two together. Or what of Proverbs 18:22, "He who finds a wife finds a good thing, and obtains favor from the LORD." Favor, then, comes from the Lord who brought this woman to this man.

Having the man set in a position over the wife in his authoritative role is often referred to being the Federal Husband. This Federal Husband is equivalent to saying that the husband is in covenant with God and his wife. A covenant is a pact or agreement between two parties that involves blessing and cursing. Here the husband is covenanted with God first, then his wife. By way of salvation, the husband and wife are equal and obtain equal benefits from Christ in salvation. But this is not by way of the family structure. Feminism today has attempted on many fronts to usurp the authority of the family structure for a liberal structure where all members of the family are on equal grounds. This may be true *salvifically*, in that Christ has saved all whom He has saved, but in terms of the authoritative *roles* of the husband over the family, or the parents over the children, this is not the case at all.

In dealing with this authority issue, one must take note that all Paul's arguments concerning the authority of the man over the wife surround Adam and Eve before the fall. Without getting too far off course here, Paul says, for example, in 1 Timothy 2:12-13, "And I do not permit a woman to teach or to have authority over a man, but to be in silence. For Adam was formed first, then Eve." In other words, before the fall, and before sin entered the world, Adam was head over Eve not only in the family structure, but even in his demonstration of that authority in, 1) being the Federal head of all mankind in the fall (men fell when Adam fell not when Eve was seduced) and, 2) Adam named Eve demonstrating his God-given power of dominion over her. Reader, take note, again, this was *before the fall*. It is a creation ordinance God set in place, and that Adam exercised and Eve faithfully partook.

Love is manifested by the husband to the wife in a number of areas. The husband loves his wife in a wise preservation of his headship and authority over her. Husbands who relinquish their authority to their wives are sinning against the express command and structure of God's ordained manner of marriage. If the wife is overpowering, and the husbands allows it, he is sinning (and consequently she is fulfilling a sinful roles of having desire to rule her husband). Proverbs 31:3 is very poignant here, "Do not give your strength to women." The idea behind this word "strength" surrounds masculinity. When men give up their masculinity to a woman, she gains power over him, thus becoming the dominant role. She gains his masculinity when he acquiesces and gains her femininity. But wives that see a loving administration of authority are glad to be in subjection to it.[2]

The husband must deal with his wife in a wise administration of his authority over her. Can husbands deal with their wives unwisely? Certainly, but this overthrows the structure and format of the marriage roles. 1 Peter 3:7 is explicit, "Husbands, likewise, dwell with them with understanding, giving honor to the wife, as to the weaker vessel, and as being heirs together of the grace of life, that your prayers may not be hindered." Dealing with them in knowledge or understanding maintains a wise preservation and administration of his authority over them. This means the husband must understand how to deal with his wife in a loving manner. Knowing how to deal with her is to mimic the manner in which God deals wisely with His church. Wisdom is the right application of knowledge. Love demonstrated in wise preservation and administration of his authority mimics Christ's selflessness in His humiliation. Christ gave His own life for the glory set before Him, but lead captivity captive and gave gifts to men. 1 Peter 2:21 says, "For to this you were called, because Christ also suffered for us, leaving us an example, that you should follow His steps..." This is very interesting that in just a few verses later Peter begins speaking about subjection, and how wives and husbands relate.

The husband has to demonstrate, outwardly, his love by example. It should be unmistakable not only by the wife, but by others in the household, or interconnected with the household, that the husband loves his wife dearly. His love will be exercised in a clear demonstration of his own biblical judgments concerning her. These are those actions toward her that he believes to be most prayerfully right. God has gifted the husband

---

[2] See how this occurs in the next chapter when the role of the woman is taken under consideration.

with the necessary abilities to make wise choices on behalf of the family unit. But such choices must be exercised wisely, and by way of understanding. This may even entail her judgment on certain matters he needs help with as well. Her opinion, counsel and observations on any given situation are considered. If the husband is very wise, then a godly concern for the decision made by the children as well may be suitable to the question at hand. But in considering all these things, the decision being made are accepted or rejected by the Federal Husband who must answer to God for all decisions being finalized on behalf of the family. It is still the husband's decision ultimately. The wife, in this way, takes no credit for her husband's exercise of authority.

The husband must also act in love to his wife in every situation. This love is an *inward* entire affection for her. The way a husband *thinks* about his wife will ultimately be seen in the manner he treats her outwardly. In this "thinking," he is to accomplish three things: he is to be chaste, pure and constant in his affection.

Chaste means that he will be innocent of unlawful sexual intercourse, or lust with anyone else. Proverbs 2:17 is clear, the adulterer and adulteress is the one who "forsakes the companion of her youth, and forgets the covenant of her God." Being pure in thought and act follows 1 Thessalonians 4:35, " For this is the will of God, your sanctification: that you should abstain from sexual immorality; that each of you should know how to possess his own vessel in sanctification and honor, not in passion of lust, like the Gentiles who do not know God." And also Proverbs 5:15-19, "Drink water from your own cistern, and running water from your own well. Should your fountains be dispersed abroad, Streams of water in the streets? Let them be only your own, and not for strangers with you. Let your fountain be blessed, and rejoice with the wife of your youth. As a loving deer and a graceful doe, Let her breasts satisfy you at all times; And always be enraptured with her love." God has providentially given this *one* woman to the husband and he is to think only of her sexually. And in turn, her sexuality should satisfy the husband at all times.

Love to the wife manifests itself in the manner of his thought life as pure and free from moral fault or guilt. The husband has no hidden agenda or manipulation going on in the marriage. He holds nothing against her, and does not manipulate her in speech or action. To "manipulate" is to twist and deceive, or practice what Paul says in Galatians – witchcraft (cf. Galatians 5:20). His dealings with her are to be pure, thoughtful, and without manipulation. Malachi 2:15 is very explicit in this, "Therefore take heed to your spirit, and let none deal treacherously against the wife of his youth."

Also, this marriage is constantly marked by firm steadfast resolutions or faithfulness. There should be a great mark of stability in the life and dealing that the Federal Husband has with his wife.

Stability in the home, stability in his relations, stability in affections, and stability in every area is the constant work of the husband. One might ask, "How stable is Christ for the Christian?" The answer to this is "always." The husband is to be the Christ figure of the home. How stable should the husband be? The answer, "as stable as Christ." Certainly, the husband's task is daunting! At what time can the Christian look to Christ and find instability? Never. So it is with the husband.

Loving the wife as Christ loved the church is the manner in which the husband must act. This kind of love is "immutable love". Proverbs 5:18 exhorts husbands, "And rejoice with the wife of your youth." When a couple is married they are rejoicing. When they are old they should still be rejoicing at deeper levels of social and spiritual maturity with one another.

Not only is the love and inward disposition, but it is an outward expression to his wife. This outward love consists in taking care of her. This means he will provide for her materially. Scripturally, the husband is the material source of blessing for his wife and home. He provides not only for her spiritual well being and her soul, but also for her body. 1 Timothy 5:8 states, "But if anyone does not provide for his own, and especially for those of his household, he has denied the faith and is worse than an unbeliever." Certainly this is applied to the lazy husband. Those husbands that are lazy and slothful are worse than the heathen if they do not provide for their families. They are to provide clothes to wear, food to eat, shelter, transportation, and the like.

In providing for her spiritually (v. 29 says that he nourishes her) we have the wonderful verse in Joshua 24:15, "but as for me and my house, we will serve the LORD." Serving God is the terminology for worship. The husband is to lead his family into spiritual service before the Lord each day, unless he is providentially hindered. But, as spiritual as the husband is so the wife will be. This means that household devotions are exceedingly important (as discussed in earlier chapters). Adam relinquished that right while he was standing in the garden with his wife and he allowed the devil to talk with her and her with him. This is not the manner in which the Federal Head should act. Adam sinned in relinquishing his role. Husbands sin in relinquishing their role as spiritual heads of the home. He is to present his wife to God without spot or wrinkle, just as Christ does the Church.

The husband is also to bear and long-suffer with her infirmities and weaknesses. Imagine how quickly Christians would be devoured if Christ was not longsuffering for the common sins of the Church. Christ keeps His people from ultimate danger and harm, and sanctifies the Church by His Word. The husband is to keep the wife from all danger and harm to protect her. This is part of helping her see and know that she is loved.

When the husband acts outwardly in his love to his wife, he makes demonstrations of that love to her in various ways. One way is in speech. Federal Husbands do not embarrass their wives in public. Imagine if Christ embarrassed the people of His church daily for their sin publicly in front of the heathen. This ought never to happen by a husband to his wife, or for that matter, the wife on behalf of her husband.

Outward love in physical attraction is a way of helping her and aiding her to become the best she can be as a woman. Christ demonstrates His love for the church in speech (the Word) and in action, His life, death, resurrection and present intercession. The husband, when he esteems his wife, loves his wife and is physically attracted to her outwardly, is a kind of "cherishing" (cf. v. 29). This love should be done in a capacity that mimics the husband loving himself. Such love is sacrificial. This kind of love will express itself ultimately in private. The Greek word actually denotes, 1) to warm, keep warm 2) to cherish with tender love, to foster with tender care. These are the poetic ways of whispering the "sweet nothings" (which are really "something") in her ear. It is the close intimacy that the husband overflows with toward his wife in private, which in turn may turn (but not always) into a sexual union.

The wife is to be honored in public before others, not belittled or humiliated. This is the manner of how they are treated or spoken of in front of others. Such a love is free and true and he that does not love his wife cannot bring but great misery and pain upon himself as accountable to God. A keen acknowledgement of his close relation with his wife being joined to her and one flesh should demonstrate a protective speech around other for her edification. His authority should never overpower the good-natured cleaving he has with her. His authority, in other words, should not be exercised at the expense of "caring for his own body." Caring for her moves from lawful authority to tyranny and can be but a single step. This is Paul's point in not abusing one's own body. Abusive husbands are not husbands and do not act like husbands. They are double minded men who have forgotten or rejected their duty as one who must care for his wife as he does his own body. They forget that marriage is patterned after the indissoluble nature of Christ and His body. Marriage is to reflect that. Why? The wife and husband are *one*. God has bound them together by covenant and by physical union. They are not only spiritually one, but physically one. And the husband must keep in mind that the manner in which he treats his wife is the manner of his own abuse or non abuse to his own body – her. Does Christ abuse His body? Never. There must remain a proper balance between authority over the body and the care of the body.

Application of the Ideas Surrounding the Federal Head

How do we as Christian husbands in our own mind live up to the expectation, no, the *command* of loving our wives as Christ loves the church? It is too often that selfish motives rule our affections at the expense of building up the body we have as one flesh with our wives. Where do we place our wives in action, in practicality, in our list of important things to do? If we were to give our wives a test as to our faithfulness in fulfilling our duties to them, what would we score? It does not matter, so much, what we think we have done. Rather, it matters *first* to God as to whether or not we have acted like Christ to our wives, and then secondly how we have acted toward our wives. Is it more *painful* to live with us than *joyful*? What kind of atmosphere do we build up in our homes and around our wives? Would our wives say "I have such an uncommon union with my husband (one that is rare in this world) in such a way that drives me to delight in him more." That is different than saying "I love my husband."

What is weighed in the balance? What does God expect of us? We protect our bodies against infections and illnesses and try to eat right and exercise and build it up – work out diet, etc. Christ does this with the Church in protecting her from everything harmful, and the Federal husband is to do this with his wife. We are to do everything we can to build up resistance to the things of the world and things that would intrude on our duty towards our wife. We should be building up our wives by our speech, by our action, by our demonstration of love, by our stability, by our spiritual direction, by our material sustenance that she is protected from world. The body needs food, the body needs exercise, the body needs understanding of how it works. The husband cares for his body, as Christ cares for His body, the church. The body needs certain things to survive. So do our wives. Yet, every "body" is different. And wives do not come with a manual. As Federal husbands, we must be keen to make our wives our life-study so that we can enable them and nurture them as they should be to grow into the woman that Christ desires.

How do you build her up? Maybe your wife has a particular weakness – what are you doing to help her overcome it? Her weaknesses are your duties. Maybe she has "special characteristics" that are annoying? Those characteristics and their eradication are not her primary responsibility but *yours*. What is your reaction to her annoyances? Are you quick to condemn her, or are you wise to enable her to over come it gracefully? Dr. Martyn Lloyd Jones said, "Do everything you can to safeguard her from the weaknesses and the infirmities and the frailties; as you do so for your body, do so for your wife." Do you talk to her? Not vent to her. Not patronize her.

Tell her about your worries in a manner that does not make her worry. Tell her about your business in a manner that enlivens her respect for you. Tell her about your secret sins in manner that prompts her to pray for you. *There is the wise husband.*

Women need to talk. It is the wise husband who knows how to communicate with her to build her up, and uses that mode of edification to make her better. How do you fulfill her needs that can only be obtained and fulfilled by your actions? If we were speaking about the union and work of Christ and the Church we would have lots of answers to questions like these. When we have to apply this to ourselves and our relationship with our wives, even in this brief (yes brief) overview, we fall miserably short. The answer to our shortcomings is not to say we will repent, but to demonstrate loving our wives as Christ loved the church.

No doubt in all this, the Federal Husband has great responsibilities over the wife. How well do you take on the responsibilities? How well do you please Christ by being like Christ for your wife? How does she think about what how you treat her? "[The wife] was not taken from the head, to show she was not to rule over him; nor from his foot, to teach that she was not to be his slave; nor from his hand, to show that she was not to be his tool; but from his side, to show that she was to be his companion."[3]

Without a true biblical reformation of the family beginning with the federal head of the family (the husband) it will be impossible to see individual family members in both their walk and duties before God and one another thrive and grow. These members will then have little if no impact on the church at large. The true biblical reformation of the husband is one of the greatest catalysts of reforming the church. When the husband

---

[3] John Angell James, *Female Piety* (Morgan, Soli Deo Gloria: 1995), 8.

is reformed, then the family is reformed, and then the family unit affects the reformation of the church. Such a reformation is for the glory of God, and then, the church as a body is reformed in order to affect change in the world it resides.

"It is a mercy to have a faithful friend that loveth you entirely to whom you may open your mind and communicate your affairs. And it is a mercy to have so near a friend to be a helper to your soul and...to stir up in you the grace of God."

-Richard Baxter, A Christian Directory

"If thou art a man of holiness, thou must look more for a portion of grace in thy wife, than a portion of gold with a wife; thou must look more after righteousness than riches; more after piety than money; more after the inheritance she hath in heaven, than the inheritance she hath on earth; more at her being new born, than at her being high born."

-Thomas Brooks, Unknown Work

8

Duties of Wives

Ephesians 5:22-33, "²² Wives, submit to your own husbands, as to the Lord. ²³ For the husband is head of the wife, as also Christ is head of the church; and He is the Savior of the body. ²⁴ Therefore, just as the church is subject to Christ, so let the wives be to their own husbands in everything. ²⁵ Husbands, love your wives, just as Christ also loved the church and gave Himself for her, ²⁶ that He might sanctify and cleanse her with the washing of water by the word, ²⁷ that He might present her to Himself a glorious church, not having spot or wrinkle or any such thing, but that she should be holy and without blemish. ²⁸ So husbands ought to love their own wives as their own bodies; he who loves his wife loves himself. ²⁹ For no one ever hated his own flesh, but nourishes and cherishes it, just as the Lord does the church. ³⁰ For we are members of His body, of His flesh and of His bones. ³¹ "For this reason a man shall leave his father and mother and be joined to his wife, and the two shall become one flesh." ³² This is a great mystery, but I speak concerning Christ and the church. ³³ Nevertheless let each one of you in particular so love his own wife as himself, and let the wife see that she respects her husband."

This section of Scripture is set in the context of the edification of the body. It surrounds submitting to one another before God. From here Paul moves into the Christian family which is finished and completed in chapter 6 verse 9. He is making a very specific contrast between Christ and the Church. Christ is the Head of the church and the church has a specific role before Christ as His body. In the same way, the family unit, which is made up of husband and wife, is set against the parallel of Christ and the Church. Wives are subject to their husbands, as the church is subject to Christ.

The argument is posed as interlaced between husbands and wives and between Christ and the Church and it is very interesting that Paul does not treat husbands first, but wives. He is dealing with a hierarchy, and the subjection of inferiors to superiors. Wives are inferior to their head, the husband, which means they are in subjection to their husbands. This is likened to the church which is inferior to Christ, which means the church is in subjection to Christ.

However, wives are the most *eminent* of inferiors in the hierarchy of the family, and so Paul deals with them first.

In order to understand this special relationship between husband and wife, one must first understand how Christ and the Church relate. By way of reminder, Christ is the Federal Head of the Church. Paul says in Ephesians 5:23, "as also Christ is head of the church; and He is the Savior of the body." Being the Head of the Church, or the representative on behalf of the Church as so dictated by the Triune Godhead, Christ governs, protects, preserves, and provides for the church., In this way He is the Savior of the Church (v. 23). He loved the Church and demonstrated that love in giving Himself up for the Church.

Christ's love for the church does not stop at simply His death and resurrection for her, but is also applied in His intercessory power in her sanctification. He sanctifies the Church by the Word. Paul says in Ephesians 5:26, "... that He might sanctify and cleanse her with the washing of water by the word..." By the various means of the application of the Word, the church is made whole. Its spots are washed away and she becomes more beautiful.

In acknowledging the rightful place of Christ, and in receiving the power of Christ's work in her, the Church submits to Christ in all things. It is, of course, a necessary subjection since the church is inferior to the Head of the body. But in this subjection, the Church is demonstrating that she respects Christ in all things. Thus, not only it is necessary, but it is voluntary. A voluntary subjection is a cleaving to Christ. In this the wife mimics the relationship of the Church to Christ. As the wife leaves her family and cleaves to the husband, so the church leaves world and cleaves to Christ. In this parallel, the wife and the church are analogically the same.

The wife, like the church, is to be subject necessarily and voluntarily to Christ in all things. What is subjection? What does it mean to be subjected to someone else? The dictionary definition means, "To make (as oneself) undergo or endure the discipline and control of a superior." In order for wives to act like the Church does before Christ, Paul lays down two commands to explain this. The first is "as unto the Lord..."

The wife is to be in subjection to the husband as if the husband is Christ. Now, the husband may not always act like Christ, and this is a sad affair for any wife who desires to serve her husband. Obviously a gentle and caring husband, though one of masculine protection and provision, would be a joy to sit under subjection. But this subjection is not accomplished by the wife simply because the husband is her husband, but because the subjection performed is accomplished as if it is done to Christ (as unto the Lord). This is the way the Church is subject to

Christ. The wife's subjection is likened to the church's subjection as the church performs its duty to Jesus Christ out of loving thankfulness for His work in and through the church.

The second part of the command that Paul lays down is that
the wife is to be subject as unto the Lord, "in everything." This
is certainly a necessary subjection if it is done to the Lord, and
in everything she does. The wife is inferior to her husband in
respect to hierarchy and position in this manner. This command is a result of the curse in the garden. Remember, Eve
was cursed by God in that God cursed *Adam* by declaring *Eve's
subjection*, but the fall would render that subjection difficult
because her desire would be to rule over her husband. No
doubt, God was in a sense, creating an irony. As Adam allowed
the woman to take up his role in the garden, (by allowing her to
deal with the serpent instead of taking up his role to protect
her) so God made this part of the curse.

In this second part of the command, "in everything", though
it is necessary, like the first part, it is also voluntary. A voluntary subjection is a most holy subjection. This demonstrates a
"dutiful respect" which inferiors have for people set over them
by God. This is why Paul says "submit yourselves" to one another in the lead-in of the passage. "Submission" is basically
saying the same thing as "do all your duties to those I have
placed over you."

Though the wife is to be subject to her husband as unto the
Lord, and in all things (everything), the loving husband makes
this a joy for the wife. Think of Christ and the Church. Does
Christ make loving Him difficult? Not at all. Christ makes
serving Him a joy to the church. Christians are enthusiastic to
serve Christ in sincerity. He loved them enough to save them,
and they love Him back in return in their service as living sacrifices. There is no other place they would rather be than serving
Christ. The wife, in this same manner, should love to serve her

husband in all things, as if she is serving the Lord. As the husband makes this joyful in his consideration of her and her work, she is pleased to love him in the necessary and voluntary subjection that God has ordained for her.

Is there a specific role the wife "plays" as wife? Yes. The Bible gives us a number of aspects that demonstrate the role of the wife. She has one husband that she follows; one husband that God has placed over her. She has a faithful subjection to him, but only such a subjection that she is subject to the Lord. Ephesians 5:22 says, "Wives, submit to your *own* husbands, as to the Lord." However she subjects herself to her husband, it must also be the same kind of subjection that it is to the Lord. She not only serves her husband, but she serves him as if she was serving God. Now, although fallen husbands would sometimes like to think so, the husband is not a "little" god" to her. Not that the husband is "a god", but that she voluntarily submits herself *to God through her husband*, and necessarily submits to him as a superior placed over her by God. Whatever God would approve of in her role of being a "wife", so she submits.

However, a word of caution is to be brought here. The wife never submits voluntarily to ungodly actions or directions. She always submits voluntarily to godly actions and affections. Ungodliness is not something that Christ desires of His people. Rather, He desires they are cleansed by the Word from all ungodliness. So no word from a husband that is ungodly is something the wife must necessarily or voluntarily follow. Instead, she is required to follow the Lord in everything. If the husband mimics the will of God, and guides his wife to follow his will as it is befitting God's will, then the wife is to be subject in all things. This is not the same, as will be shown, that the wife "disagrees" with the husband on a certain issue. Rather, this revolves around her subjection to a "godless" command. In such instances, she is never to obey or be in subjection to evil.

Wives who do not subject themselves to their husbands are in rebellion against God, not simply in rebellion to their husbands. Strong willed, rebellious wives are not simply rebelling against the word and will of their husband, but they are rebelling against the will of God that requires them to be in subjection to their husband. Sometimes it is very hard for a woman to be in subjection to her husband, especially in the 21st century with "women's lib" and "independence" constantly bombarding the media and airwaves. But the godly wife will see that as an attack on the family, and God's ordained means of glorifying Himself in the midst of the family unit. She will reject it and follow her husband as to the Lord in all things.

Things to Learn from the Text

In thinking through what is most important in this text concerning true biblical reformation in the role of the wife, the duties of the wife are of prime importance. The duties of the wife are seen in her subjection to her husband as to the Lord, as both necessary and voluntary. However, in this act, the subjection which is required of a wife to her husband implies two things: 1) she acknowledges her husband to be her superior, and 2) she respects him as her superior.

In dealing with acknowledging her husband as her superior, two aspects should be noted. First, she acknowledges the husband's superiority as general of any husband. Secondly, she sees this particular of her own husband. Exploring this a moment will be of great help in the manner in which a wife treats not only her husband, which she is obliged to submit to, but her disposition to "husbands" of any kind.

Husbands have a number of titles in the Bible. These titles show his superiority and authority. He is called "lord" and "master"(1 Peter 3:6), "guide" (Esther 1:17), "head" (Proverbs

2:17), "the image and glory of God" (1 Corinthians 11:3, 7). Why does the husband have such "eminent" titles? The husband represents Christ on earth to his wife. The wife, then, represents the relationship the church has with Christ. William Gouge, in his work *Of Domestical Duties*, says, "A wife's outward reverence towards her husband is a manifestation of her inward due respect of him." This is wholly true. As the Christian's heart demonstrates his love for Christ, so the inward affections of the wife demonstrate her love and subjection to her husband.

In seeing the intent of the heart of any wife towards her husband, her inward disposition can never be discerned by her husband, or those around, simply in and of itself. The husband can only view the good disposition of the wife towards him, and her affection for him, in manifesting an outward reverence for him. Reverence is summed up as *affections born out of respect*. Such reverent gestures to him are very important in the unity between husband and wife.

What is a *reverent* gesture? What can a wife "do" to demonstrate this? 1 Peter 3:12 says, "Wives, likewise, be submissive to your own husbands, that even if some do not obey the word, they, without a word, may be won by the conduct of their wives, when they observe your chaste conduct accompanied by fear." Here, the apostle Peter says that she must have a *willingness* to be under him and ruled by him. There should be, then, a desire to honor him in her actions. This means, for example, that the way she dresses before others on behalf of her husband is important. Her speech and how she talks about him to others, or in front of others, is of importance. Respect for his authority is seen in her confiding in him, as in 1 Corinthians 14:35, "And if they want to learn something, let them ask their own husbands at home." Even in the speech she uses to address him, in her sweet disposition of him, is seen as in 1 Peter 3:5-6, "For in this manner, in former times, the holy women who trusted in God also adorned themselves, being submissive to their own husbands, as Sarah obeyed Abraham, calling him lord, whose daughters you are if you do good and are not afraid with any terror." This kind of husband, or master, is not a dictator to her, but lovingly governs, protects, provides and preserves her, and she reciprocates this by her reverence for him.[1] A wife is also to have a meek and quiet spirit as characteristic of her disposition towards her husband. Peter instructs her when he says in 1 Peter 3:3-4, "Do not let your adornment be merely outward arranging the hair, wearing gold, or putting on fine apparel rather let it be the hidden person of the heart, with the incorruptible beauty of a gentle and quiet spirit, which is very precious in the sight of God."

In following all this, it is impossible to deny that there is a "scriptural station" for the wife as wife in relation to both Christ, as her Lord, and her husband, as Christ's vice-regent to her on His behalf. These various duties are outlined very well in the characteristics of the wife of noble character of Proverbs 31:10-31. It would be wrong to skip over Proverbs 31. It would equally be wrong to not fully explain the text and its importance for the wife. But since there are many other works out there that take time to consider Proverbs 31 alone, here we will simply overview the chapter.

The text of Proverbs 31 begins, "Who can find a virtuous wife? For her worth is far above rubies. The heart of her husband safely trusts her; so he will have no lack of gain." This surrounds the moral quality of the wife. As verse 12 states, "She does him good and not evil all the days of her life." The place where she does this good is "the home." This is evident

---

[1] As a note, it does not take long to discern how a husband is treating his wife after talking with a hurting wife. How she speaks with others demonstrates the husband's faithfulness in loving her as he ought.

also from Titus 2:35, "the older women likewise, that they be reverent in behavior, not slanderers, not given to much wine, teachers of good things that they admonish the young women to love their husbands, to love their children, to be discreet, chaste, homemakers, good, obedient to their own husbands, that the word of God may not be blasphemed." Such a wife is also industrious, as in Proverbs 31:13-16, "She seeks wool and flax, and willingly works with her hands. She is like the merchant ships, She brings her food from afar. She also rises while it is yet night, and provides food for her household, and a portion for her maidservants. She considers a field and buys it; from her profits she plants a vineyard." She is strong in every sphere of her life. Verses 17-19, "She girds herself with strength, and strengthens her arms. She perceives that her merchandise is good, and her lamp does not go out by night. She stretches out her hands to the distaff, and her hand holds the spindle." She is mindful of every area of the home. Verses 21-24 and 27, "She watches over the ways of her household, and does not eat the bread of idleness....She is not afraid of snow for her household, for all her household is clothed with scarlet. She makes tapestry for herself; Her clothing is fine linen and purple." The husband is part of the home though he may be away from the home, and through her husband and the work she accomplishes for him, he is respected. Verses 23-24, "Her husband is known in the gates, when he sits among the elders of the land. She makes linen garments and sells them, and supplies sashes for the merchants." She is spiritually minded in her work. Verses 20, 25-26, "She extends her hand to the poor, Yes, she reaches out her hands to the needy. Strength and honor are her clothing; she shall rejoice in time to come. She opens her mouth with wisdom, and on her tongue is the law of kindness." She is respected for her diligence and capability. Verses 28-29, "Her children rise up and call her blessed; her husband also, and he praises her: Many daughters have done well, But you excel them all." It would be a great sin for the husband of such a wife to go around silent about a wife of noble character. Shame will be brought on every husband who has not so verbally and outwardly express such a kindness and respect for his wife. Even her children know how great and awesome she is in God's eyes – she is called blessed by them. As a result of all this that she accomplished, there is a commentary at the end which says in verses 30-31, "Charm is deceitful and beauty is passing, but a woman who fears the LORD, she shall be praised. Give her of the fruit of her hands, and let her own works praise her in the gates." Let the husband boast scripturally of his industrious wife. Let him supply her with everything she needs, and she will be praised by him in the gates. Why is this so? She is a *godly* wife. She fears the Lord. Everything she does is unto the Lord – for she does all in godly fear.

In briefly looking at the wife of noble character, the wife in this respect is a *help meet*. Without the wife, the initial cultural mandate in Genesis to have dominion over the earth is impossible. But, the wife must have a likemindedness to the decisions of the husband for the cultural mandate to be successfully enacted. Husbands that lead dictatorships will always press the wife to exasperation. Husbands do not need slaves, they need helpmeets and wives who are stationed accordingly, and follow the wise and loving leadership of their husbands. Wise leadership will create mutual harmony.

What if a wife does not want to be a wife of noble character? At that point there is a far greater problem occurring – rebellion against God. The neglect of her duties demonstrates rebellion against her husband as to the Lord and demonstrates she despises her position. For a wife to give up her duties, or never take up her duties as an industrious wife falls under one of four categories: first, that she has a wrong conception of what Christ requires as a wife. She does not know what to do, or has never been taught God's will for the wife. Second, she is married to an unbeliever and her duties are hindered and neglects those duties for safety. Unbelieving husbands may find her spiritual leadership appalling, so they neglect it for sake of peace. Thirdly, her husband is exasperating her and she gives up her duties. Unwise and uncaring husbands, or wrongly motivated husbands, can easily exasperate their wives into non-action. The wife looses respect for the husband, and becomes physically and emotionally distant, and her duties as a wife suffer. Fourthly, the wife simply does not approve of God's plan for the wife, and remains in open rebellion against Him. The wife should be sure (being truly informed by God's word and desiring reformation in her marriage) that which she refuses to do at her husband's command, is forbidden by God, otherwise she is bound to the duties the Bible gives her as a wife. The wife must maintain that duty to the husband which is duty to Christ. But it must be remembered that such duty is done either joyfully, as a result of the husband's loveliness in the eyes of the wife, or with grief, as a result of being married to someone who is really a fool. Yet, in any case, the wife is bound to her husband and holds duty to him as to Christ.

How the Text Applies to Us Today

How is the family reformed towards true biblical reformation by your godly involvement in the home? As a wife, how are you subject to your husband as to the Lord? Is it hard when you as a wife have to look into the face of your husband and see Christ there, especially if your husband is not acting in accordance with what Christ would do, or in the manner in which Christ would do it? Imagine for example, that your husband is exasperating and consistently demonstrates to you your habitual sins. Now, rightfully, he should be helping you overcoming those sins as Christ would help the church, but he must be wise in doing so. Yet it is your duty, as Christ commands, to yield meekly to your husband's critique. Remember, 1 Peter 3 says that you must have a gentle and quiet spirit. That is not a spirit of a lackey; rather, it is a gentle and quiet spirit. It will be hard to subject yourself to your husband if you regard him as a tyrant, as a dictator, or as a fool. You must first truly understand that your husband requires your respect simply because he is stationed there as your head, as Christ is head of the church. It will be easy to subject yourself to him if he is loving, wise, faithful, etc. as we discussed in the traits of the husband. The wife of noble character has no qualms with a husband that acts like Christ. As the church is in love with Christ, so the wife is in love with her husband. But, the loved wife, who is cared for by a husband that resembles Christ, will be ready to subject herself to him as she is designed to. You would never use a blow-dryer to bake cookies. It is not designed that way. If you were really patient, you may be able to cook them if the blow-dryer was hot enough, but really, who in their right mind would try it? It is not the way cookies are to be baked. It was not designed to work that way. Wives are designed in such a way that in such mutual circumstances, there is a cultivated desire to submit to the husband. But there is no grading on a curve with easy or hard as becomes the duty of the wife, or husband. You must still fulfill your role as if you were serving Christ regardless of how loving or unloving your husband acts to you.

Take time to consider how you react to your relationship with your husband. Are you the model wife? Would he call you the wife of noble character or the industrious wife? Would others? So much depends on your role as wives, and even as mothers, that the foundations of the church are strengthened by your work as a wife and the duties that you fulfill. Think about that – your duties as wife are a means by which the

church of Jesus Christ is strengthened and true biblical reformation comes to pass. Instead of focusing in on your husband's
weakness, sins and problems, first be sure to look at what you
are to be doing *yourself*. Does your husband trust you? As a
wife, how are you fulfilling your duties? All are sinners, but
Scripture presses our roles to cause us to consider how well we
accomplish what God gives us to do.

We cannot simply say, which is the common expression, "I
fail all the time, so I'll just try my best as a result." No where in
the Word of God do the Scriptures ever give any Christian that
option. (Ministers hate to hear that because really it is just an
excuse.) You have to consider what is most important. For the
wife, the household on behalf of her husband is most important. This cannot be emphasized enough. Whatever else may
be hanging over your head, nothing is more important to the
wife than fulfilling her responsibilities to her husband and to
her home, as unto the Lord. Other people, other activities, other business are not your first priority, *EVER*. At no time is
pleasing others ever more important than what is pleasing to
your husband. At no time is accomplishing works for others
ever more important than accomplishing all that is required of
your husband. Duties outside of the home, in general, are a far
third or fourth rung on the ladder of life to the primary duties
of the wife to the husband as if done to Christ. Not even your
local church is more important, since Christ has providentially
given you a husband, not a church, to serve as wife.

Single people attend the Lord and Him only, and as a result
have a greater focus towards God in their service to Him. Husbands and wives attend each *other* as unto to the Lord. They
have a bit more pressure since they not only serve Christ, but
they serve Christ through serving one another every day, day in
and day out. When your husband gives you a duty to perform
that is not against the Word, or any inferences from it, you are

to engage it as the industrious wife. Neglect of it is sin. It is against the commandment to disobey him since wives are to respect their husbands and to be subject to them (Ephesians 5:33). Is the church saddened at Christ's commands? Not for the regenerate mind. Is the wife saddened at her husband's commands? Not if dealt with in love. Yet even simply as accomplishing it as a duty, it must be done.

All that is owed by the husband to the wife will be enhanced and cultivated as they live in Scriptural harmony with one another. As a wife, how are you willfully neglecting your duties? Are you disrespectful to him? Are you kicking against the goads to his *biblical* wishes? Among other means of maintaining an inward loving affection between man and wife, outward mutual peace and agreement is one of the most principal acts of love they can show to one another. Are you in agreement with him in everything? And if not in everything, then at least subject to him in respect? Does he know you are subject to him and respect him in this way? Are you conscious of his role as Christ? An easy way of assessing whether the relationship between husband and wife is Scriptural, is whether or not *the husband praises the wife at the gates*. Christ boasts of the church.

Is the husband so satisfied with you as a wife that he praises you at the gates? Reflection is worth its weight in gold for every wife that takes the basics of such exhortation to heart to be subject to her husband as unto Christ.

Though these biblical guidelines are vitally important, they are impossible without the help of God and in the grace and power of the Holy Spirit. None of this is accomplishable without Christ or without His grace. The husband cannot love his wife and the wife cannot be Scripturally subject to and have respect for her husband without grace. The importance of such matters can be easily weighed in our own hearts as to how much we pray for such things. These are the very basics. At the very least, these ideals should press us to study, since the basic principles are set forth for the husband and the wife in the Bible and in these passages. Without heeding them, the family will never move on to true biblical reformation. And if the family is not reformed, the church will never be reformed.

"The parent is the only teacher who is permitted to stand at the beginnings of human life, and to shape the first thought which arise in the mind."

– Dr. B.M. Palmer, *The Family in Its Offices,*
Instruction and Worship

"Great reason there is why this affection of love should be fast fixed in the heart of parents towards their children. For great is that pain, pains, cost and care which parents must undergo for their children."

– Dr. William Gouge, *Of Domestical Duties*

❧ 9 ❧

Duties of Parents

Ephesians 6:1-4, "Children, obey your parents in the Lord, for this is right. ² "Honor your father and mother," which is the first commandment with promise: ³ "that it may be well with you and you may live long on the earth." ⁴ And you, fathers, do not provoke your children to wrath, but bring them up in the training and admonition of the Lord."

It must be remembered that these exhortations toward reforming the family are set in the context of the edification of the Body. This is theme the reader has been reminded of for three chapters now. However, it is vitally important. The family affects the church. If the family is truly reformed, the church will reform. Paul began in 5:22 and will continue until 6:9 which completes the context of submission to one another. It is the central theme here before God. From the edification of the church, he moves into the edification and submission (or roles) of those in the family. He speaks about the submission of the husband to God, the submission of the wife to the husband, and the submission of the children to the parents. But though he speaks about the children's submission to the parents, in this chapter the role of the parents over the children (to keep in step with the family reforming by the parents lead) will continue.

The reformation of the family not only consists in the relationship of the husband to the wife, but also from the parents to the children and the children to the parents. As the text states in 6:1,

"Children, obey your parents in the Lord, for this is right." Who is he addressing? The answer is "children". Literally, they are the offspring of the parents, those born under authority. The word "obey" which is

The Greek word *hoopakoo'o* means "to listen, to hearken" and refers to "one who on the knock at the door comes to listen who it is." This is the duty of the porter. Porters listen carefully to answer knocks on the front door in order to fulfill their roles as "guards" of sorts into the home or house. More generally obedience is something done to superiors out of obedience to them. This particular obedience to parents by their children comprises every kind of obedience that could be rendered. Paul does not give specific commands, rather, they are to generally obey their parents in every command.

Parents are the designated God-ordained superiors over children. Because children are bound to their parents, the duties which they perform are not of courtesy, but of *necessity*. Their parents have power to command, and exact from them whatever they deem physically and spiritually beneficial before God. Why is such obedience necessary? Paul gives the qualification of "in the Lord." This demonstrates a check, course, and establishment for the child. It is a check showing that children's obedience to their parents is to be restrained to the obedience which they owe to Christ, and may not go beyond its limits. It is a course showing that in obeying their parents, they must have a watchful eye to Christ, and so obey their parents as if Christ would approve of all their actions, or not. It is an establishment of their duty showing that parents bear the image of Christ, and in that respect children must obey their parents because they are, in fact, obeying Christ.

Why does Paul tell them they should obey their parents? He says, "...for this is right". This is the way it should be because obedience to parents fulfills the fifth commandment. In every point of the law, or righteousness (which is really the same as saying they are reflecting the character of God in righteousness), it is right to do. Since parents bear the image of Christ's authority, it is lawful for children to obey them. If they do not obey them, they are rebelling not only against their parents, but against Christ's authority. As it is their duty to obey Christ, it is their duty to obey their parents.

It is just and right to obey parents because God has instructed children to do so. In this way Paul exhorts covenant children when he says, "Honor your father and mother," which is the first commandment with promise". The commandment here comprises under it all those duties which inferiors owe to their superiors. It is a command that not only deals with mothers and fathers, but the manner in which relationships work between those superior to those inferior. This concept is annexed to the command and not only a reasonable inference, but a necessary one. This is the fifth commandment, which is the first part in the second table of the law which is a summary of our respect to all superiors annexed to the command. The *Westminster Larger Catechism* in question 124 asks, "Who are meant by father and mother in the fifth commandment"? The answer is, "By father and mother, in the fifth commandment, are meant, not only natural parents, but all superiors in age and gifts; and especially such as, by God's ordinance, are over us in place of authority, whether in family, church, or commonwealth." Not only does the commandment house immediate superiors, but also those annexed to the command: *any* superiors or inferiors. The *reason* annexed to the Fifth Commandment is a promise of long life and prosperity (as far as it shall serve for God's glory and their own good) to all such as keep this commandment. To keep this commandment is an appeal to temporal prosperity. This is very interesting since Paul is dealing with children on the level of children. How do you talk with children? Paul is wise in using not only the duty to be performed, but the benefit of the duty when it is performed. If children obey their parents, there is the hope of a reward.

In verse three, Paul makes a short commentary on the previous statement when he says, "that it may be well with you and you may live long on the earth." Paul is expounding the commandment stated in Deuteronomy 5:16, "Honor your father and your mother, as the LORD your God has commanded you, that your days may be long, and that it may be well with you in the land which the LORD your God is giving you." How would this be applicable in the 21st century church? Does this commandment really count with covenant children today? Is the commentary relevant? Well, the "land" is shifted to be "the church" in regards to covenant community. For example, 2 Chronicles 7:14 states, "if My people who are called by My name will humble themselves, and pray and seek My face, and turn from their wicked ways, then I will hear from heaven, and will forgive their sin and heal their land." This verse is not a reference for the church today to be content with real estate, or that America will somehow be blessed. The covenant community (land) in the Old Testament, is the same covenant community (synagogue or church) in the New Testament. Covenant children are included in this command and have a particular warrant to understand temporal blessing in the home and covenant community. Paul is exhorting them to live long. This is the substance of the command, and differs from the "circumstance" of the command which is the physical location, whether in Canaan or in a church service. It implies long life, and prosperity in their own inheritance before the covenant members of church. As Paul exhorts in other places, such as 1 Timothy 4:8, "For bodily exercise profits a little, but godliness is profitable for all things, having promise of the life that now is and of that which is to come." Well being in this life is a covenant blessing. Or consider Genesis 28:20, "Then Jacob made a vow, saying, "If God will be with me, and keep me in this way that I am going, and give me bread to eat and clothing to put on so that I come back to my father's house in peace, then the LORD shall be my God."

How is long life a blessing? Living life creates opportunities in time for God to minister to children and to others through them. God is not just concerned with children as children, but as children who grow up into useful parents and adults. That is why Paul does not simply say "you will be blessed", but rather, "you will have a long life." That is the essence of the command. Children will grow up into useful adults. All of this, then, is pointing towards their own good in their sanctification. Psalm 34:12 is very clear on this, "Who is the man who desires life, and loves many days, that he may see good?" Not only is this long life good for the child, but it is also for the good of others in the church, and for God's glory in all things that the child completes as "godly seed" through life on behalf of God. Paul exhorts the church in other places irrespective of age when he says in Galatians 6:10, "Therefore, as we have opportunity, let us do good to all, especially to those who are of the household of faith." God so orders his favors and blessings to the good of those on whom he bestows them. He desires that they prosper by them. The appeal, then, is really to self-interest. If children truly want to be blessed, and blessing only comes from God, then self-interest is the best tool to use to motivate children in obeying their parents. This is Paul's (or rather the Holy Spirit's) logic in the matter.

In verse four Paul makes a further connection between parents and children, "And you, fathers, do not provoke your children to wrath, but bring them up in the training and admonition of the Lord." The parents, through fathers, should take such care of their disposition toward their children, as they give them no occasion to be stirred up to wrath. Fathers should never "provoke" their children to be angry with them. The parent should be a model of stability. Exasperating the child tells the church something about the nature of the inward instability of the parent which may demonstrate itself in immaturity.

The word "bring up" signifies "to feed". This is like the text in Jeremiah 3:15, "And I will give you shepherds according to My heart, who will feed you with knowledge and understanding." Feeding is set in the context of eating good things. In Jeremiah's case it was sound doctrine. In the case of parents and children, because of the lack of maturity in children, parents, who should be much more mature than their children, should be *aware of that lack of maturity.* Children are much more fragile, and easily exasperated. Instead of exasperating, they should feed them or "nurture" them, which means "correction and instruction". Parents are to nurture them, correct them, and instruct them. This applies to their physical, mental and spiritual well being. All this revolves around the constant admonition to the child to live a holy life before God as a covenant child, and later, as a covenanted adult. Without that continual "catechizing", true biblical reformation for the children in families will never occur. Proverbs 22:6 is very clear, "Train up a child in the way he should go, And when he is old he will not depart from it." Children need instruction to follow and a path to walk. This is not something they do only out of duty, but out of voluntary necessity. Children cannot simply be "dutiful children", which is answering "what they should do", but also instructed children, as to how to accomplish any task best. God is not looking for children to be slaves, but covenant children that will be useful to the Kingdom as they grow up. These, as Malachi 2:15 states are godly seed, "He seeks godly offspring."

How the Text Teaches Us Important Lessons as Parents

What is most important to pull out of this text and section of Scripture to be applicable to children? Children are to obey and honor their parents as if they were obeying and honoring God. This is most important. If children disregard the teaching of their parents, then true biblical reformation of the home will break down, and the church will cease after a generation or two to be reformed. How the families of the church would live in greater harmony and spiritual peace if their children understood this. Parents are authoritatively placed over them and are to be obeyed by that necessity. The very basics of the commandment teach this. It is the duties of parents to their children to nourish them physically, nurture them with correction, and instruct them in the ways of God. In this way, though the parent desires duty and conformity from the child, everything the parents do is bound up in love. Titus 2:4 says, "that they admonish the young women to love their husbands, to love their children," Genesis 22:2 makes plain, "Then He said, "Take now your son, your only son Isaac, whom you love..." Though parents are to love their children in their raising of them, they should also be very careful not to love their children too much and spoil them. Can a parent love their child too much? When parents make their children idols, and spoil them, and not discipline them, they have crossed the line and have sinned not only against God, but also their children as well. They cannot have a love towards one with love towards all, or show impartiality to children, even if one son or daughter is more obedient than another. They are to love them with a sincere love in Christ as a parent should love their children. An unbalanced love, or a spoiled love, can cause great problems for both the children and the parents. Take this as a lesson in Genesis 37:4, "But when his brothers saw that their father loved him more than all his brothers, they hated him and could not speak peaceably to him." Not only is it not grateful to God to love all the children of a household equally, but it causes dissention in the home.

It is important to nourish children physically taking proper care to provide things that are needful for their life and health. The parent's role in this begins in the womb, and is completed when their children are married. In Judges 13:4 why was the charge of abstaining from wine, strong drink, and unclean things, given to Manoah's wife? It was given by God as a result of the child who was in her womb.

Think about the disrepair that women take on their children even from the womb. There are drug addicts who smoke crack, do drugs of all kinds, drink alcohol, eat excessive nutritionally deficient foods and the like. Instead, the biblical picture is to nourish and care for the child from the moment he or she is conceived, until they are married and sent off to cleave to their own wives and husbands.

It is even important, contrary to popular culture, that in marriage the Bible consistently demonstrates the parent's responsibility in finding godly wives and husbands for their children. Jeremiah 29:6 says, "Take wives and beget sons and daughters; and take wives for your sons and give your daughters to husbands, so that they may bear sons and daughters that you may be increased there, and not diminished." Should not the godly parent take a primary role in being sure the help-meet of their children are biblically sound, honorable and godly? When parents neglect this, they neglect their children's well-being, and to neglect their well-being is to sin both against their children, and against God who has given them over as stewards of their children before Him.

It is important that even down to the good manners that children have, their parents are training them respectfully. Paul says in Romans 13:13, "Let us walk properly, as in the day, not in revelry and drunkenness, not in lewdness and lust, not in strife and envy." William Gouge in his work *Of Domestical Duties* says, "Rude bringing up makes children to be of a crooked, perverse, stubborn, churlish, surly, doggish disposition; as on the other side, good nurture in this kind breeds ingenuity, amiableness, courtesy, and kindness."[1] Again, this is an echo of Proverbs 22:6, "Train up a child in the way he should go, And when he is old he will not depart from it." If a parent neglects this, then they have to deal with Proverbs 29:15, "The rod and rebuke give wisdom, But a child left to himself brings shame to his mother."

Though a parent trains up their children in the way they go , they must take the necessary steps in order to nurture them with correction. Raising children is hard. It is wearisome to consistently raise them and discipline them. Paul knows that men and women grow weary of doing good, even though it is good that they do it! He says in Galatians 6:9, "And let us not grow weary while doing good, for in due season we shall reap if we do not lose heart."

The parent must take the time to reprove the children and follow through to discipline them so that they will obey as they ought. The Bible speaks plainly about this. There are many passages throughout the Scriptures for reproof and correction of children. Proverbs 19:18 says, "Chasten your son while there is hope, and do not set your heart on his destruction." In like manner Proverbs 29:17 states, "Correct your son, and he will give you rest; Yes, he will give delight to your soul." And Proverbs 23:13 commands, "Do not withhold correction from a

---

[1] William Gouge, *Of Domestical Duties*, 592.

child, for if you beat him with a rod, he will not die." Proverbs
– the book of how not to foul up the proper growth of your
child – is important to heed since it is deemed God's "wisdom
literature." To be wise would be to listen to the wisdom of the
Word in correcting children as God intends.

Contrary to the duty of correcting children are two extremes
that must be avoided. One is too much leniency, which demonstrates that the parent spoils the child. The other is too much
severity, which Paul warns about in exasperating the child. Instruct them in the ways of God, is a good sign of a parent's concern for the welfare of their children. Their spiritual disposition before them will be of the greatest importance in the manner in which the child mimics their parents. Do they pray for
them? "The promise is to you, and to your children" (Acts
2:39). Parents should pray with a great assurance that they
may call on God on behalf of their children for His blessing.
God's promise is the ground of faith: so far as God's promise is
extended, so far our faith may and ought to extend itself.

Parents should have a desire to pray for God's blessing on
their children in all things. Job was a character in this manner
as seen in Job 1:5, "So it was, when the days of feasting had run
their course, that Job would send and sanctify them, and he
would rise early in the morning and offer burnt offerings according to the number of them all. For Job said, "It may be that
my sons have sinned and cursed God in their hearts." Thus Job
did regularly." They key here is the word "regularly." Parents
should never be thinking about the outward state of their children (clothes, looks, vanity of any kind) before they are utterly
consumed with the inward state of their children and their
eternal salvation. Many times parents are far more concerned
about what their children will wear, or eat, or their inheritance,
than they will about whether or not their children will spend
eternity in heaven or hell. This obviously rolls over into the spi-

ritual manner in which the parent raises the child.

True Biblical Reformation in the home begins with covenanted *families*. Thus, placing the sign of God's covenant on
them at the proper time is the starting point to following
through in raising them as godly seed. *The Westminster Confession of Faith* in chapter 28:5 says, "Although it is a great sin
to contemn or neglect this ordinance..." In other words, to neglect spiritual duties surrounding children, like covenant inclusion, is a great sin. Even Christ said in Matthew 19:14, "Let the
little children come to me and do not hinder them, for to such
belongs the kingdom of heaven." Little children (covenant
children) own the Kingdom of God. It belongs to them. They
should be treated as such. Raising them under the preaching
and teaching of the Word in church and in the home is of utmost importance, but it always begins with covenanting. The
duty of the Federal Head is to raise up his family like a little
church, which means a covenanted oath is essential to the right
disposition of the parent's spiritual understanding of his child
before God. Parents, then, ought never to treat their children
like pagans do, and neglect the sign of the covenant placed
upon their children as their inauguration into the visible
church. Then, after their inauguration, comes their catechizing.
This is essential for their growth in the Bible and in theological
ideas contained in the Bible but expressed clearly and memo-
rized. The Reformed Faith in its ethical consequences on the
family involves their spiritual training. *The Westminster Directory for Family Worship* says, "The ordinary duties compre-
hended under the exercise of piety which should be in families,
when they are convened to that effect, are these: First, Prayer
and praises performed with a special reference, as well to the
publick condition of the kirk of God and this kingdom, as to the
present case of the family, and every member thereof. Next,
Reading of the scriptures, with catechising in a plain way, that

the understandings of the simpler may be the better enabled to profit under the publick ordinances, and they made more capable to understand the scriptures when they are read; together with godly conferences tending to the edification of all the members in the most holy faith: as also, admonition and rebuke, upon just reasons, from those who have authority in the family". In the family a parent is "all in all" over his child: a king, a priest, and a prophet. Therefore anything a parent believes the church must do for their child in instruction, the parent is more duty-bound to accomplish that at home first. This takes time, and many years of faithful training. But God is patient. Study of the word is as Isaiah 28:10 teaches, "For precept must be upon precept, precept upon precept, Line upon line, line upon line, Here a little, there a little." Little by little they are trained and brought up in the fear and admonition of the Lord that they may grow into godly seed.

How the Text Equips Us to be Good Parents

How well are you raising your children? This chapter was not simply an exhortation to children to obey their parents, but how parents are to raise those children in light of the command of God upon them and their children. Christian parents have the responsibility before God to raise godly children, not to drive them further away from God. Our job as parents, or even extended parents as we have leave to have an impact on the children around us, is to create and influence children to be godly seeds. Parents themselves have a keen interest in raising their children in a godly manner, but because of the fall, it is easy to become exasperated with their behavior, or their degree of maturation. What kind of impact do you have on children?

Have you ever noticed that God is exceedingly concerned with orphans through the bible – children are very important – they are the future. Malachi 3:5 says, "And I will come near you for judgment; I will be a swift witness against sorcerers, against adulterers, against perjurers, against those who exploit wage earners and widows and orphans, and against those who turn away an alien because they do not fear Me," Says the LORD of hosts." James 1:27 says that, "Pure and undefiled religion before God and the Father is this: to visit orphans and widows in their trouble, and to keep oneself unspotted from the world." Raising godly seed is of prime importance to God. That is because children are little mimics – they will do what they see you do, and they are always apt to do more sin than righteousness. For example, Abraham lies about Sarah as his wife, and so does Isaac – like father like son. A parent's responsibility, then, is first before God as a good example to raise their children in a way that honors God. Then they are to be good parents. You must demonstrate the righteous character of Christ to your children in the way you live, walk, talk, act, sit, sleep, eat, pray, attend church, read Scripture, have devotions, and everything in between.

You as a parent have a choice whether or not to honor God in the way you raise your children, or to reject God's plan for a godly seed and raise a child after your own image. Either we are made continually into the image of Adam, or we are made into the image of Christ. I do not mean that we are made, as in "formed in the womb", this way, but as it refers to the way we influence and are influenced.

Fallen men and women continue to create beastly children who follow their example and their moral stature. That is why the world is so terribly dysfunctional, and that families all over the planet are dysfunctional. How dysfunctional are they since every family is affected by the fall, and what are they doing to correct it? God has set a certain temperament and rule for parents to raise children so that they are trained up in the way they should go, not the way they would go. They would become as

Cain, Lamech or Jezebel without the godly checks of God's intellectually stimulating revelation to us in the Scriptures.

Oftentimes, because of sin, our own society is made up of children that are raising children. Instead, though, children are suppose to be raised by physically, mentally and spiritually mature parents who have a desire to fulfill God's mandate on what God expects of children and their relationship to their parents. Your first response as parents is to ask what God expects of you as a parent, not what feels or seems good to you. Christian parents do not follow the trends of the world in raising children, instead, they look to the time-tested precepts of the Word to guide them. That is where your authority lies. It does not lie in yourself, but in your transmission of God's precepts. You are to exercise authority over your children. Is this obvious? For some, not really. As parents, you are really required to be very good biblical counselors and teachers. That means that when raising your children, you are a student of the psyche and a counselor who knows how to bring together biblical wisdom with a cool, calm and collected attitude in any situation that your child may bring you.

We often hear of the "terrible twos", or the spoiled four-year old, or the teenage rebel. But the Scriptures are not lying to us. God is not lying to us when He says, "train up a child in the way he should go"...and maybe he will follow your lead? No. If you train up a child in the right way, he will never depart from what you teach him. That presupposes a right way and a wrong way of training up a child. And that is the ultimate point of the proverb. This is why Paul says to fathers that they ought not to exasperate their children. Fathers should know how to deal with children and what God expects of them to do so, that they may grow up to be useful adults. How are you training up, nourishing, nurturing, and disciplining your child? Right? Wrong? Indifferently? By the standards of the world? It will not take long to see who runs the house and how well they run the house. Is the child training you up, and exasperating you? Are you simply flying off the handle and exasperating them? With young children it can be, in certain ways, hard to discern how well catechizing, or bible teaching, is working. For example, the child prays, but how much of that is actually impacting him or her just yet?

The reformation of the *child* is the key – to change them from being beasts, fallen like their father Adam, to being godly seed. As parents, you are duty bound to discipline, nourish and train your children for their good. *Loose, undisciplined raising of children will always drive children away from God.* That we know. Raise up children without Biblical instruction, and God may give you your wish of allowing them to run freely into the arms of the world. Leave them alone – that is all you have to do. Just the idea of the constant watch is tiring. Dr. Spock, Dr. Phil and Oprah are not trusted guides for raising children. New Age techniques will never replace continued supervision and spanking. Giving your children over to anything not commanded of you in Scripture for their wellbeing will never be blessed by God.

Children are under your God-given authority. Do not let them win in the battle. I have heard mothers say, "When I count to three, if you have not done it, you will get spanked – One......two.......two and half...." Now understand, the child won once the mother started bartering. Children should obey upon your first command. They should obey without challenge, without excuse and without delay. If they do not, they are prime candidates for a good spanking. Follow Proverbs 23:13, "Do not withhold correction from a child, For if you beat him with a rod, he will not die." This is the same idea as Deuteronomy 24:20, "When you beat your olive trees, you shall not go over the boughs again; it shall be for the stranger, the fatherless, and the widow." This is not exasperating as if out of frustration or anger, but with a godly discipline. That means that you as a parent regulate your children's character and you use godly discipline to do that. That does not make daddy a monster when he disciplines his children every ten seconds; it makes him *godly*. Who is boss? Them or you?

In *The Little Book of Christian Character and Manners* by William and Colleen Dedrick, there is a wonderful list in the back that are warning signs for parents who do not have authority in their home, or a signal that they are loosing control in their home. Here they are:

- My child whines, cries, and pouts when I say "no" to him.

- I find myself reluctant to ask my child to help with any tasks because of his negative reaction and inability to complete a job. He usually responds to my requests by whining or answers, "I can't...or I don't want to..."

- There is an excessive amount of noise and confusion in my house: screaming, bickering, crying, hitting, rough behavior with furniture or toys, etc.

- I am unable to leave food snacks or any-thing of personal value within my child's reach.

- I am unable to leave my child (aged three or above) out of my sight or unattended in another room for any period of time without being worried about what he is up to.

- I am embarrassed or afraid to take my child to other homes or the restaurant because he is so active (boisterous, silly, fidgety; he knocks things over and touches every-thing).

- My child is unable to sit quietly for any length of time in a place I specify.

- Going shopping is a fiasco because my children run through the clothes racks, or touch everything in the store, or run away from me.

- My child has a "smart mouth" (yells, uses abusive language, swears at me) or hits me.

- My child throws tantrums, refuses to eat or do what he is asked to do.

- My child takes things without asking and rummages through our drawers and cupboards.

- My child does not come when called or respond to my voice from another room.

- When I ask my child to do something I always have to explain "why" first.

- Many of my child's toys are broken and he rarely puts any away—outdoors or indoors.

- My child avoids doing what I ask by using flattering words, changing the subject, or doing some other good deed instead.

- My child gets my attention with loud, disrespectful demands, e.g., "Hey, Mom! Get the __ for me!" or "I want __ !" or "Mom, come here!"

- I find myself saying, "I can't do that because Suzy won't let me" or "I can't get Johnny to do that..."

- When I spank my child he pouts, responds in anger, screams, throws himself on the floor, slams doors, prolongs his crying, coughs, or gags (attempts to vomit).

- As I talk on the phone or chat with others, my child constantly interrupts or acts naughty, demanding my attention.

- My child is constantly bored, discontent, and looking for entertainment; wanting to play, he grumbles at his work.

- I am ready to pull my hair out. My child drives me crazy. I am so worn out all the time that I can hardly wait to get a break from him at every opportunity.

How sharp is your Scripture memory? Can you think of a verse dealing with each of the above? These are examples of poor character qualities that the Bible— especially Proverbs— addresses.

But you must be warned – never to crush them, never to smother their spirit, never to be overly harsh. Your children are immature. You must always remember this. It is God's intention that you mature them. This is true biblical reformation of the home.

As we follow God's plan for the relationship between parents and children, God will bless our work with them. They will, in turn, affect the home, church and society in the way you raise them. Will they be godly seeds, those that obey their parents? Or will they rebel? If you are looking for true biblical reformation in the home, then follow the Scriptural mandates for being faithful covenanted parents for covenanted children.

"A Christian is a perfectly free lord of all, subject to none. A Christian is a perfectly dutiful servant of all, subject to all."

- Dr. Martin Luther, The Freedom of a Christian

❧ 10 ❧

Workplace Reformation

Ephesians 6:5-9, "Bondservants, be obedient to those who are your masters according to the flesh, with fear and trembling, in sincerity of heart, as to Christ; 6 not with eyeservice, as men-pleasers, but as bondservants of Christ, doing the will of God from the heart, 7 with goodwill doing service, as to the Lord, and not to men, 8 knowing that whatever good anyone does, he will receive the same from the Lord, whether he is a slave or free. 9 And you, masters, do the same things to them, giving up threatening, knowing that your own Master also is in heaven, and there is no partiality with Him."

Its imperative in dealing with this particular section of Scripture that the reader continues to remember that the exhortations to each family member is set in the context of the edification of the *church*. The church, though, extends not only to the family, but also *society* in general. This then presses the family to affect the social sphere they influence in such a way as to create an environment in their vocation that is as equally glorifying to God. If true biblical reformation begins at church, then permeates the various offices of the family, it then, by *necessity* extends into every vocation and place of employment the Christian is able to work.

The context of this section extends from 5:22 through to 6:9. It emphasizes, in every aspect, to submit to one another; from the church, to the husband and wife relationship, to parents and children, as well as to masters and servants. Paul now moves into exhorting masters and slaves, a logical extension of familial relations as he completes his exhortation. Reformation, in the biblical sense, reaches even to slaves and masters. It reaches out into society and changes it for the glory of God.

In verse 5 he says, "Bondservants, be obedient to those who are your masters according to the flesh, with fear and trembling, in sincerity of heart, as to Christ." This title "servants" is a universal title. It revolves around any outward household, civil or right which places one under another. Servants owe their service to another. There are no exceptions here, and no loop holes. Inferiors owe obedience as slaves to their superiors. Paul places slaves and master under the family because homes in those days always had slaves, or one was a slave. Yet, in every case, in every job, the extension of the master / slave relationship moves to the employer / employee relationship on any task as will be investigated.

The master is the one to whom service is owed. This service is owed by right. William Gouge rightly says, "The rule of servants (as servants) is the will of their master."[1] Everything that servants should do is comprised in the word "obey". All tasks owed to the master by the servant, as children obey their parents, is to be performed as a duty, and as a service.

Paul says that such is done "according to the flesh". As much as a master is according to the flesh, so is a slave, but the distinction here is in relation to earthly superiors. These earthly superiors are to be obeyed "with fear and trembling". Fear is reverence, or a kind of respect that is due another. Trembling is with anxiety, but not with anxiousness. It is feel-

---

[1] William Gouge, *Of Domestical Duties*, 161.

ing as though one is about their ability to perform the task as well as one would like. It also holds the idea of "will I be punished if I do not do well?"

This obedience is done "in sincerity of heart". This is surrounding the truth and righteousness of obedience as it is done as if to Christ Himself. Slaves are subject to masters as if they were subject to Christ Himself. Colossians 3:23 says, "And whatever you do, do it heartily, as to the Lord and not to men."

In verse 6 Paul says, "... not with eyeservice, as menpleasers, but as bondservants of Christ, doing the will of God from the heart..."

Because servants may have a hard time working for masters, Paul continues to expound their duty in more particulars. "Eyeservice" can be hypocritical service. This is when someone does something that really is pretended to be accomplished instead of done in sincerity. Hypocrites are pretenders (much like the Pharisees who "pretended" in this way to be part of the kingdom of God). They look like they are working but they are not working. Such service can also be done while the master is watching, but when he is not looking. If this is the case, the slave is not working, and is in tact stealing. That contradicts the idea that slaves are to act "as to Christ" formerly since God sees everything always. God often requires more than what men will give other men.

Eyeservice often turns into manpleasing. Manpleasing is secret atheism. This is when servants or employees are more apt to please men before they are apt to please God. They are more concerned with how they look in front of men than they are before God. It does not matter to them if the job is actually accomplished so long as they look like they are accomplishing it. Again, this is a form of not only stealing, but lying. It is an act that believes God is not looking.

Paul says that slaves should act as "slaves of Christ, or

bondservants of Christ". To avoid committing such sins before God and their masters, slaves are exhorted to be slaves of Christ first, as though their masters are Christ Himself. This will allow them, then, to do the "will of God from the heart." Slaves are first to be concerned with God's authority over them as if it is God's will that they do everything as unto Christ. Such service, then would not be for men, first, but for God first and from a right heart, or motive to please God in everything they are given to do.

In verse 7 Paul says slaves work, "with goodwill doing service, as to the Lord, and not to men". This explanation carries with it an additional force or exhortation to these things. The Greek word for this *service* means *readiness* and *cheerfulness* in doing a thing; it is doing something with good or right thoughts. Such a fulfillment of duty before masters is for their masters good, and through a *godly* mind on *behalf* of their masters.

In verse 8 Paul then says, "... knowing that whatever good anyone does, he will receive the same from the Lord, whether he is a slave or free..." Here is a verse in which one must "read between the lines". If masters are not fair, or not rewarding, the slave knows that such a reward is given from God, not directly from masters. That also means that all the labor a slave puts into his work before Christ will never be in vain. He will be rewarded either in this life, or the life to come. God is faithful to reward those that diligently seek Him and work as unto Him.

Paul then says in Ephesians 6:9, "And you, masters, do the same things to them, giving up threatening, knowing that your own Master also is in heaven, and there is no partiality with Him." Paul moves from slaves to masters. Masters are now addressed so that they will perform their due service to slaves. Masters have duties to slaves? Certainly. Slaves have a due service by the very fact that masters have responsibility over them. They are required to work as unto the Lord, knowing that Christ is their master, and has far greater power to require service to them as masters, than they do slaves as slaves. But, the master's duties are set under the phrase "do the same things" – good things – in their place over slaves. Masters are not allowed in this way to think that slaves are simply for their own use and pleasure. Rather, they have a duty required of them to the slave. The master cannot think that he is greater than a slave in some way or that he has more worth than the slave. God appoints the work and boundaries of men, and masters must understand that God shows no partiality in the master over the slave. God made men what they are in their vocations. Some He makes masters, and others slaves. The master, then, has no right to lord over a slave as a dictator, or tyrant. Respect of persons is the cause of all that injustice and wrong which masters do. Thus, God is pleased when masters act in accordance to their role on behalf of salves. All this, though, is somewhat speculative unless it is placed in a context that fits its use in every respective age.

What We Can Learn About Masters and Slaves

The Reformed Tradesman, or *Slave*, owes obedience to his master as if to Christ in sincerity of heart, and will be rewarded for his labor. What is a *Reformed* Tradesman? One could say it this way: employees owe obedience to their bosses as if to Christ in sincerity of heart. That seems simple enough. If a household held slaves, or servants, such would be the case in that household as it was in Paul's day. That is why employment is set under the duty of the *home*. But the hermeneutical application of these texts for the contemporary church would more readily revolve around employees and employers. That is the manner in which our society, at least in America, works. There are, certainly, many countries where this passage with house-hold slaves would work in the exact manner that Paul is de-scribing because many cultures still have household slaves.

To have true reformation in the American workplace in which Christians live is a great need. Oftentimes, people want to work the least, for the most money. This is the epithet of the "great American workplace". However, Christ expects the Re-formed employee to be spent not only for Christ, and the voca-tion God providentially places them in, but for the masters or employers that they work for.

Employers have a particular interest that they need em-ployees to work and fulfill. Their interest is should be the em-ployee's interest. Employees owe obedience in the best interest of their masters as if they were employed by Christ. God knows man's need, especially in a fallen world, and He has so gifted men with a diversity of gifts that in any sphere or any arena men will work as slaves or masters before God first. Every one who is capable of it should be constantly employed in some use-ful station of life whether as a slave or master, an employee or employer. The Reformed Tradesman owes obedience, then, as the express command and appointment of God. Adam, before and after his fall, was placed in a state of action, or employ-ment. From the beginning men are to obey God, and all those in authority providentially over them.

Men were built to work. For some reason Christians often think that men were just made to sit around and talk about the-ology. Actually, working is *theology applied*. Genesis 2:5 says, "...before any plant of the field was in the earth and before any herb of the field had grown. For the LORD God had not caused it to rain on the earth, and there was no man to till the ground." Man was placed in the garden to *work*. He was to till the ground. Work in a pre-fallen garden of Eden was much easier and quite enjoyable than what it is in a fallen world. In a fallen world work is cursed. God cursed work as a result of the fall. God made work hard because of the fall of Adam in the garden. Though it is hard, it is very necessary. Still, men were created to *work*.

When men work, or when employees work for their employers, there are two considerations to make. One is negative and the other is positive. The negative is to abstain from doing things that pop out of their own head. This is when an employee will try to do something without or against their master's consent. The affirmative is to always be ready to yield to do everything their employers want and desire they should do.

Employers or masters have been providentially chosen by God to take up certain stations in life as sovereigns over a particular sphere. Maybe they have a service, or sell a good, or whatever. God has placed them there and given them the gifts to make that job work for the good of society. Employees have an obligation to respect them for this work, and render them due service for a fair wage. They treat their masters not as men, but as Christ. They have to, then, guard their actions to be becoming of Christ and thus to men, without eyeservice, or menpleasing. Eyeservice, manpleasing or laziness is opposite to obedience owed just a duty. As Proverbs 14:23 says, "In all labor there is profit, But idle chatter leads only to poverty." Christians must be honest and admit that idleness is stealing. "By much slothfulness the building decays; and through idleness of the hands the house droppeth through" (Ecclesiastes 10:18). "Behold, this was the iniquity of Sodom, pride, foulness of bread, and abundance of idleness was in her, and in her daughters; neither did she strengthen the hands of the poor and needy" (Ezekiel 16:49). In rejecting those avocations which would divert employees from their business, laziness results. Laziness, or hypocrisy in work, is a violation of *God's* sovereignty, of the commandments and the general obedience due towards any employer. Even after the fall this was still the case as God said, "by thesweat of his face to eat his bread, until he should return unto his dust."

Employees should never work simply to be seen for what they do – that is Pharisaical. Instead, they should work so diligently that they are recognized and then rewarded. Proverbs 18:16 says, "A man's gift makes room for him, and brings him before great men." This was the case in 1 Kings 11:28, "The man Jeroboam was a mighty man of valor; and Solomon, seeing that the young man was industrious, made him the officer over all the labor force of the house of Joseph". The exercise of one's giftedness, which is glorifying to God, is utilized for God's glory, and for the benefit of the employer and company. Yet even in this, because of the curse, sometimes being too good is a burden because more is expected. But ultimately all such work will be rewarded either in this life, or in the life to come.

It should be no wonder, then, that the Reformed Tradesmen would be the most diligent and respected worker. And such work is never conditional upon being under a "good master", but rather because the employee knows that first and foremost, he is working for Christ. In Dickens' *A Christmas Carol*, Bob Cratchet worked diligently regardless of the circumstances. Scrooge's disposition could make the job easy or hard. As one reads the book, they find Cratchet working under miserable conditions. But Cratchet was always diligent to work hard and be humble for his station in life.

Not only do employees work hard as if they were working unto Christ, but they work in fear and trembling. William Gouge says, "The other part of that fountain, from whence the duties of servants flow, rests in the affection: and it is in one word fear: which is an awful dread of a master. An awe in regard of his master's place: a dread in regard of his master's power. An awe is such a reverent esteem of his master, as makes him account his master worthy of all honour: which saint Paul expressly enjoins servants to do. [1 Tim 6:1] A dread is such a fear of provoking his master's wrath, as makes him think and cast every way how to please him. This is it which the apostle here intimates under these two words, fear and trembling."

In like manner, William Gouge says, "So proper is this fear to a servant in relation to his master, as where it is wanting, there is a plain denial of his master's place and power; which God intimates under this expostulation, If I be a master, where is my fear? [Mal 1:6] that is, you plainly show that you account me not your master, because in your heart there is no fear of me."[2] It cannot be a slavish fear. It cannot be a despising fear. Such a reverence is manifested in speech and action, and it is done as to Christ.

What does it mean that the employee works "as unto Christ"? Simply, it is done or accomplished with sincerity of heart. Richard Steele explains, "Diligence, as it relates to trade, is an habitual employment of our bodily and mental powers about our proper callings, in a just and happy medium between idleness, lethargy, and trifling curiosity, on the one hand, and slavish drudging and immoderate care on the other."[3] This is taken from the principle of Christ when he says in Luke 6:31, "And just as you want men to do to you, you also do to them likewise." If an employee owned a business, how would they want their "help" to treat them? If one were to work while Christ was standing over them, they would be industrious to the end. Paul's point the passage is that all things done in sincerity of heart, not begrudgingly, are done to Christ, and on the best interest of the employer or master for which it is accomplished.

There are four principles to sum here in all this: 1) There is

---

[2] William Gouge, *Of Domestical Duties*, 594
[3] Richard Steele, *The Religious Tradesman*, 72.

a diligence and sincerity about the work before Christ. 2) There is a diligence and sincerity about the work itself. 3) There is a diligence and sincerity about the best interests of the employer. 4) There is a diligence and sincerity for the employee as a result of the reward both temporary and eternal. Let the Christian employee be excited to the practice of being industrious in everything he does. God's blessing is on the industrious worker. The Scriptures say in Genesis 39:6, "Thus he left all that he had in Joseph's hand..." In Genesis 39:5 it is the same, "So it was, from the time that he had made him overseer of his house and all that he had, that the LORD blessed the Egyptian's house for Joseph's sake; and the blessing of the LORD was on all that he had in the house and in the field." As a result, Joseph was rewarded for his diligent and sincere labors before God. God is particular about such service when He says in Leviticus 19:13, "You shall not cheat your neighbor, nor rob him. The wages of him who is hired shall not remain with you all night until morning." Not only this, but even with an expectation of future reward by Christ.

On the other hand, the Reformed Employer, or Master, owes obedience to Christ and service as a lawful master to every employee, or slave. Masters owe obedience to Christ in a more threatening manner, with more responsibility to be reminded that Christ is their master. Employers are not better than employees; they have been simply placed in a different providential sphere as a result of their gifts and God's gifting them as leaders. Proverbs 28:21 says, "To show partiality is not good, because for a piece of bread a man will transgress." It is a "dog eat dog" world out there because of sin, not because of righteousness. Employers cannot threaten, for the same threatening they do, so their Master in heaven can do. They should be aware of their employee's gifts, talents, wages, work, etc. to use them most affectively, and to render them a fair wage affectively. Like employees, the work accomplished is not about simply "working", but how the Employer demonstrates a godly position before Christ to the employee. It is biblically wrong (morally evil) for an Employer to think about how much he can get out of an employee for the cheapest rate. This is not becoming the Reformed Employer. Neither can the Reformed Employee think about how he might do as little work as he can for the highest pay.

Fair wages, fair treatment, fair exhortation to work, knowledge of the employee are the master's business because of his station as a result of providence. Being a savvy businessman should be coupled with being a generous employer with thoughts, not simply of how much money the company will make, but how things are most glorifying to God. It is not, for the Employer, "do everything I can to make a buck." God owns all the "bucks" and distributes them as He sees fit. Employers should strive to be good stewards for God. It is the fair and respecting treatment of the Employer to the Employee before Christ that Paul stresses here. Does the church see Christ as good? Then slaves should see masters as good. They should see Employers as good to them. There should be no question as to motive or fairness.

How the Text Applies to Masters and Slaves, or Employers and Employees

Do you treat employees like family? Remember, the context is the family. Paul spent four times as long on employee as he did to employers. The average American employee wants to work as little as possible, for the most pay. The average American Employer wants to pay as little as possible for the most work. Both of these concepts are part of what constitutes the American Dream – you can have it all at little effort. Only old-time immigrants have poverty stories where they came over on the boat with $3 in their pocket and finally made it when they became manager of a grocery store, or something where they turned it around to gain the fancy car or the fancy house. From God's perspective these two ideas (working little for great pay, or, paying little for much work) are anti-biblical ideas. God says much on the worker being worthy of his wages, and the difference between the diligent industrious worker and the lazy slothful beggar. Those who want to work little for much pay are the *beggars* of Proverbs. Proverbs 21:17 says, "He who loves pleasure will be a poor man; He who loves wine and oil will not be rich." Proverbs 12:27 says, "The lazy man does not roast what he took in hunting, But diligence is man's precious possession."

Employers should be ashamed of themselves for attempting, in their own debased minds, to gain as much as they can while paying out as little as possible to workers who are worthy of their wages.

Say an employer in a grocery store has two employees, one which is exceptionally gifted and the other not so gifted, but a friend of the owner. The friend is paid double what the gifted one is paid, and the gifted one is relied on more because of his gifts, and yet is paid less because the owner thinks "I am a shrewd business owner who is smart with his money". There are two faults in this thinking (not to mention it is godless), 1) it is not "his" money – it is his stewardship of God's money and 2) it is a form of extortion. In both cases employees and employers need to take some biblical lessons from Paul's exhortation – Christ is your master, treat your inferiors and superiors as if you were treating them as Christ Himself.

The Bible clearly demonstrates that men should work. "And Abel was a keeper of sheep, but Cain was a tiller of the ground," Gen 4:2 (cf. 1 Samuel 16:22, 17:15). Psalm 104:22-23 says, "When the sun rises, they gather together And lie down in their dens. Man goes out to his work and to his labor until the evening." Working diligently with sincerity of heart is godly action at work.

Working should give way to ministry. Acts 9:36 states, "At Joppa there was a certain disciple named Tabitha, which is translated Dorcas. This woman was full of good works and charitable deeds which she did." Also, Acts 20:34-35, "Yes, you yourselves know that these hands have provided for my necessities, and for those who were with me. "I have shown you in every way, by laboring like this, that you must support the weak. And remember the words of the Lord Jesus, that He said, 'It is more blessed to give than to receive.'" Paul previously exhorted the Ephesians in 4:28, "Let him who stole steal no longer, but rather let him labor, working with his hands what is good, that he may have something to give him who has need." He also instructs Timothy and Titus. 1 Timothy 5:13, "And besides they learn to be idle, wandering about from house to house, and not only idle but also gossips and busybodies, saying things which they ought not." Titus 3:8, "This is a faithful saying, and these things I want you to affirm constantly, that those who have believed in God should be careful to maintain good works. These things are good and profitable to men." You must ask yourself then, how good of an employee are you? Industrious, reverent, working with fear towards your master as to Christ? Or, are you after the dollar?

Reformation of the workplace would revolutionize society. It did for John Calvin and Martin Luther. By these two men, through the power of the Gospel, capitalism was profoundly affected for the good of society. Honest business all around was part of their goal for the good of society to the glory of Christ.

Maybe you have a scornful master, or employer. God's sovereignty does not discriminate. God has placed that employer over you. One can never forget that the way they treat their employers is how God will ultimately recompense them in this life and in the life to come. There are rewards for godly service. God will move employers to respect their employees, as he moved Ahasuerus to recompense the faithfulness of Mordecai (Esther 6:3). If masters fail in this duty, God will even move strangers to recompense them just as He moved the jailer to favor Joseph when his master had cast him in prison (Genesis 39:21) and Pharaoh to advance him to great dignity (Genesis 41:40).

God will even so providentially situate a diligent employee that the employer's heart will be drawn more to them. In this God will make the things which they labor in to prosper. He did this with Joseph (Genesis 39:2) and Abraham's servant (Genesis 24:56). In dealing for themselves God will bless their work, as He blessed Jacob's while he was in the house of Laban (Genesis 30:43). If it that one day the employee will become the master or employer, God will, provide employees for them as they were to their masters. In Egypt God blessed Joseph with a faithful servant (Genesis 43:23). David, who did everything he could to save his father's sheep (1 Samuel 17:34) had many servants that did everything they could with their lives for him (cf. 2 Samuel 21:17; 23:15). Within this same idea is applied the words of Christ in Luke 6:38, "For with the same measure that you use, it will be measured back to you."

Masters or Employers, how good of an Employer are you? God is very strict with Employers or Masters. Luke 16:2 says, "So he called him and said to him, 'What is this I hear about you? Give an account of your stewardship, for you can no longer be steward." Employers should be intimately aware of everything that goes on with their employees. It is their stewardship. Stewardship on behalf of God implies *knowledge*. Employers must know all about those they are serving in their respective role as a master. Yes, Employers serve employees in a different sense than simply by a work or due to them. They still owe godly obedience to Christ on behalf of the employee in order to be the best Employer they can on behalf of Christ.

Employers are bound to supply the temporal necessity and wages of the employee. Not only are Employers to pay the current wages, but they are to plan for the employees future. Deuteronomy 24:15 says, "Each day you shall give him his wages, and not let the sun go down on it, for he is poor and has set his heart on it; lest he cry out against you to the LORD, and it be sin to you." "When shall I provide for my own house?" says Jacob to his master Laban (Genesis 30:30). This rhetorical question shows that this is a master's duty. Are you too hard, too soft, negligent, and ignorant? Are you too stingy? Remember Luke 10:7, "...for the laborer is worthy of his wages". This is a universal labor precept. Couple this with Ecclesiastes 9:10 and you have a great Employer in action, "Whatever your hand finds to do, do it with your might." Does this only apply to slaves? Certainly not! It applies to masters as well. We must reform the way we think about work, and what God's intention is in putting us to work and creating us to work before we can work rightly. How will true biblical reformation take our workplaces by storm when people are often following the American Dream instead of the desires of their God?

"Time is a talent given us by God. He has set us our day, and it is not for nothing."

- *Jonathan Edwards, The Preciousness of Time*

❧ 11 ❧

Redeeming the Time

Ephesians 5:16, "...redeeming the time, because the days are evil."

In dealing with "Biblical Reformation" we have covered the reality of true reformation, and various stations in life where Reformation needs to take place. However, knowledge itself is not enough. The Christian must take advantage of the time God gives him to engage in reformation, or the principle of reformation will be meaningless. That is why covenanting is so important. It presses the Christian to act based on a solemn vow he makes to God. "Whosoever taketh an oath ought duly to consider the weightiness of so solemn an act, and therein to avouch nothing but what he is fully persuaded is the truth."[1] Christians can agree that Reformation is good, and necessary, but unless they are taking advantage of the time God gives them to enact it, then it is simply theory.

The short verse in Ephesians 5:16 is set in the context of community or church edification. It surrounds the specifics of "submitting to one another" and instructs the Christian com-

---

[1] *The Westminster Confession of Faith*, 22:3.

munity, the covenanted community that desires true biblical reformation to redeem the time. Regardless of what station one is in the family, or the covenant community, this text applies not only to those stations, but the manner in which those stations are exercised. In this passage is something for everyone. It is an exhortation for all, excluding none.

Ephesians is the house built out of theological bricks, and in it there is a theology of *walking*. Ephesians 2:10 says, "which God prepared beforehand that we should walk in them." Ephesians 4:1 says, "I, therefore, the prisoner of the Lord, beseech you to walk worthy of the calling with which you were called..." Ephesians 4:17 says, "This I say, therefore, and testify in the Lord, that you should no longer walk as the rest of the Gentiles walk, in the futility of their mind..." Ephesians 5:2 states, "And walk in love, as Christ also has loved us and given Himself for us..." And again in Ephesians 5:8, "For you were once darkness, but now you are light in the Lord. Walk as children of light..." Then in Ephesians 5:15, "See then that you walk circumspectly, not as fools but as wise..." For the purposes of the text at hand that fits so nicely into this theology of walking, Paul says "See then..." The Greek here forms a transition to the cardinal matter. Remembering the pagan ways these people used to dwell in, now they are to renounce them. Walking in the futility of pagan ways in rebellion against God is to waste precious time. To go back to walking in that way is a waste of precious time. Time, for the Christian, is precious. It is never to be wasted and always to be redeemed. All that he had just named in the previous verses, as a result, do the following. Paul is saying, "...see that you do this."

What is it that Paul desires the Christian to do? He says, "...that you walk circumspectly..." Paul says "walk". He does not say run. He wants the Christian to walk circumspectly. Wisely. Thoughtfully. He wants the Christian to mind himself in his walking. This is much like a teacher at an elementary school simply telling the children to walk slowly to the lunch room so they will not trip and fall. There is, then, an exhortation to diligence and care, not speed. The exhortation does not revolve around "eating lunch" though. The matter that Paul is addressing is much more important than simply eating lunch. Run from sin, the flesh and the devil, but until they rear their ugly heads you are to be like a game hunter who is careful in their search for prey. That is why Paul uses the next word "circumspectly". This means "exactly, accurately, and diligently." The worse and more corrupt that the ways of this world become, the more watchful the Ephesian Christians ought to be in every situation, and give regard to nothing but the will of God found in the Scriptures. They are to be so exact, accurate and diligent in their walking that they use the utmost precision to complete the task they have. But, Paul does not tell them how to do this just yet.

Paul then uses a description of those which walk circumspectly. Those that walk rightly walk "not as fools, but as wise." Wisdom is the right application of knowledge. This is not just to have knowledge but to use it in a proper and godly way. Walking is a godly action, but it is not simply walking for the sake of walking, rather, it must be done in right action.

Paul then exhorts them to always be about "redeeming the time." To walk in a way of wisdom means to redeem the time (cf. Ephesians 2:10; 4:1; 4:17; 5:2; 5:8). In this passage, there is the final and climactic theology of walking. The tense is "imperfect" in the Greek and means "do it and never stop doing it". It is an action that begins, then continues for all time. It is a command to walk, and to walk in a certain manner. Literally it means "to buy up the time," as if one was in the marketplace and has a very keen eyes for business. Those with keen eyes in the marketplace always find the best deals in shopping.

For the Ephesian Christians, Paul is exhorting them to see time as invaluable, seizing each opportunity to the glory of God. What is time? Time is an instance or single occasion for some event. Time is the half dimension of moment to moment that always moves forward. It is a definable moment based on what is occurring during that moment. A birth of a child is a series of moments that could take 36 hours. A sneeze is set within a short moment. In Paul's exhortation, time is an event made up of moments that define the event. Reading the Bible may take one person one hour and another person 30 minutes to read the same passage. Praying may work the same. One may pray for an hour, another for an hour and a half. But in any set of moments or any single event, for the Christian, it must be redeemed.

Why must the Ephesian Christians redeem the time? Paul says "because the days are evil". The Greek word here is *ponaros* which means, "wicked or bad in an ethical sense". These redeemed people, once being godless and wicked, know the days are evil because they had been partakers of those days. They know what evil is, and what it looks like. However, instead of partaking in evil deeds, they must have a different viewpoint than that of the pagan. They must be wise, not fools; walking circumspectly, not running, but careful. They must take back time and rescue it from foolish use. In this way Christians should set a high value, and be exceeding careful that time is not lost. Christians, therefore, are exhorted to exercise wisdom and circumspection, in order that they may redeem time effectively. And so the Apostle demonstrates that time is exceedingly precious to the Christian.

What the Text Teaches Us About Time Redemption

God commands that Christians ought always to see "time" as invaluable. It must be realized that every moment a Christian spends on the earth is invaluable time. God values time. Christians ought to value what God values. Genesis 4:3 says, "And in the process of time it came to pass that Cain brought an offering of the fruit of the ground to the LORD." Numbers 9:2 states, "Let the children of Israel keep the Passover at its appointed time." Ecclesiastes 3:1 says, "To everything there is a season, a time for every purpose under heaven." Galatians 4:45 is exceedingly poignant here, "But when the fullness of time had come, God sent forth his Son, born of woman, born under the law, to redeem those who were under the law, so that we might receive adoption as sons." From the eternal decree of God, the Lord sets special consideration when to accomplish His goals. Throughout the entire Bible God opens divine revelation in a particular and most careful manner, step by step progressively. Jesus came wrapped in the sphere of time at a particular point in time to save His elect people. It is in time, this sphere, that every Christian lives and moves and has their being in God in Christ. This, living before this God in time, and using time wisely is an invaluable opportunity that the Christian has to glorify God and live acceptably before Him.

Time is a gift of God. God is not obliged to give people any more time than they have now. Ecclesiastes 3:2 says there is, "a time to be born, and a time to die." Rare commodities cost much because they are seen as precious and are oftentimes scarce. So time is of like rarity and very special. The time that is passing now will never be here again. The time Christians spend doing what they do, then, should be of utmost important and in pursuit to glorify God. Every breath sucked into our bosom is a gift. The Christian must treat it as it is, a gift of God. Anything given to a Christian by God is invaluable. Time is simply a limited gift needful of being wisely used. The word itself, "time", has an emphasis of limitation. This is not like those who think they have "all the time in the world to be

saved." Time is a rare commodity. There is much of it, however, it is passing and fading. Christians ought always to engage in *time redemption*.

God redeems the time, so should every Christian. From the
beginning, God set six days to work and one day to rest. God
takes special consideration of the time He spends in the work
He has to do. Even in this Paul says in the beginning of the
chapter, Ephesians 5:1, "Be imitators of God..." Christians as
imitators of God ought to always redeem the time. It is impossible to read through the life of Christ and not see every act,
every moment, and every word of Christ as a model of time redemption. The worldly man will say, "I have all the time in the
world." But he is deceived. God commands time and may require the end of the worldly man's time when He so chooses.
The Christian, though, has been enlightened. Christians ought
never to find a second of time when time is not redeemed.
Time should be continually redeemed. Christians are, in fact,
the only ones who can redeem time because they follow the divine dictates of God, and God has made them alive in Christ to
please Him. They desire to fulfill the divine commands in holiness, and they desire to please God in everything they do.

Why should Christians always be about redeeming the
time? Biblical reformation is a constant day in and day out action. Reformation never ends. Thus, the time it takes to redeem the time is exceedingly important and valuable. And
Christians know that they must always "redeem" the time, because the days are evil. Even now, in the time of the 21st century church, the days are as wicked just as much or even more
so than in Paul's day. Though sin may abound in any age, it
seems there is more to distract the Christian today through
modern technological marvels. Distractions of any kind are
hindrances to redeeming the time. The Christian is wise who
knows this, compared to the unbelievers who do not know this.

When someone says, "Times aren't so bad," this shows a foolish, unsaved mindset. Time passes moment by moment and it is a commodity which will never come again. The wicked generation consumes time as if they have an endless supply of it. But they do not realize that 1) they cannot get back what they squandered, and 2) God is in control of their very breath. At any time He can end their time here on earth.

Time-redemption can never be from the past, but time-redemption must always be in the "now". Once time is lost, it is gone forever. It is not like the ball game when the team is down three points, and it is in the last inning, that the heavy hitter comes up to bat and redeems the game. Rather, Christians must be "walking circumspectly" "wisely" in order that time is not wasted or squandered. The whole game counts in the eyes of God, not just the last swing of the batter. Christians must never, then, act out of accordance of being time-redeemers. They can never afford to walk in any other way that circumspectly, and wisely. They cannot ever be in a daze. In old campy horror movies, zombies walk around trying to wreak havoc on small towns, or on unsuspecting archeologists who dug up their tomb and disturbed their rest (It is hard to believe that is attractive entertainment). They are often categorized as mindless slow-walking dead men who are simply animated for a time. They are often easily stopped by the "smart humans" who save the day. Christians can never act like walking zombies. The reprobate are walking zombies. They disregard redeeming the time because they are not aware that they should even make the most of time unless it be for their own self reasons. Christians, instead, should be lucid and circumspect in everything they do, right down to eating lunch in order to glorify God (1 Corinthians 10:31). When time is gone, it cannot be regained. Children who neglect their parents in such a way as to mind their own privacy often wake up later in life, when they hit fifty, and are reminded of how bad they treated their parents, who are now deceased, and wished they could gain that time back to redeem it. But it is gone, and time should never, ever be wasted.

People do not realize that for both the Christian and the unregenerate, there are eternal consequences in "time-redemption". Rewards and punishments for time-redeemers and time-wasters will come to full light in the last day when Christ will judge men's works.

Ecclesiastes 3:17 says, "I said in my heart, "God shall judge the righteous and the wicked, for there is a time there for every purpose and for every work." The Apostle Peter says in 1 Peter 1:17, "And if you call on the Father, who without partiality judges according to each one's work, conduct yourselves throughout the time of your stay here in fear."

How Time Redemption Applies to True Biblical Reformation

Do you believe time to be invaluable? What kind of price do you put on time? How important do you see your use of God's gift? People say, "Don't waste my time!" All of it is God's time and not simply your own time. You are on borrowed time from God. True biblical reformation will never occur for the glory of God unless you are reminded that it is God's time and His agenda that you should be striving after. 1 Corinthians 6:19 says, "Or do you not know that your body is the temple of the Holy Spirit who is in you, whom you have from God, and you are not your own? For you were bought at a price; therefore glorify God in your body and in your spirit, which are God's." If you are now bought with a price, and have to honor God with your body, then everything you do is important in whether or not you are wasting *God's time*. "Are you wise, not as fools?" The Holy Spirit said that people in this way are either "fools" or "wise". Do you practice Time-Redemption with God's time? God has not given us a time machine to fix our errors and reenact lost time. Time goes by without our consent. We cannot retrieve the time back after it has gone by—we cannot redeem lost time. But the affects of what we did with our time continue until the affect is built upon or remedied. Did you make a mistake? It cannot be undone, but you can correct the future ramifications of your mistake. Did you sin? You can ask forgiveness. Did you hurt someone? You can go and be reconciled. The mistake, sin or hurt you did will never be taken away since it is something that is record for all eternity in time-past. But the affects of its outcome can be remedied, which is what should be done if you are really redeeming the time. If you have sweet communion with Christ, then further that communion and redeem the time toward biblical reformation in powerful prayer. Are you caught in an engrossing sin that seems to escalate each day? Then redeem the time in forgiveness and remove yourself from the triggers that cause you to sin. Instead, though the principle of wickedness attempts to pull us away from righteousness, we should be redeeming our time well and with godly intention. Remember, there are eternal consequences to time-redemption.

The Lord Jesus never squandered his time. He was always engaged with His mission – to fulfill the work of the Covenant of Redemption that was given to Him to do. Luke 19:10 says, "for the Son of Man has come to seek and to save that which was lost." Mark 10:45 states, "For even the Son of Man did not come to be served, but to serve, and to give His life a ransom for many." Christ was diligent to complete that work and uphold His end of the pact and agreement made with the Father and the Spirit from all eternity. He even gave us the discernable time when He completed His task when he said, "It is finished" (John 19:30). But what about your desire to redeem time? Is it as focused and diligent as Christ's? Christ gave us the Spirit of Power to walk in the Spirit and not in the flesh. You will have to make a decision as to whether you want to be a time-redeemer or a time-waster.

For the Christian, there really is no choice. The Christian is always after true biblical reformation, and that means he is always a time-redeemer. That means you are evaluating everything you do. Everything you do in every sphere of your life should be constantly evaluated to be sure that you are not wasting time but redeeming it. You can hear the objection already - "Are you saying that we have to be conscious of every point of time that we affect?" Well, think about simply eating lunch. Does God care about how you eat a hamburger? As a matter of fact, yes He does. 1 Corinthians 10:31 reminds us, "Therefore, whether you eat or drink, or whatever you do, do all to the glory of God."

How many Scriptures do you know for idleness, slothfulness, laziness? Are you as wise as the ants? Think about it – are you as wise as that little diligent bug? Proverbs 6:6-11 is quite to point with this, "Go to the ant, you sluggard! Consider her ways and be wise, which, having no captain, overseer or ruler, provides her supplies in the summer, and gathers her food in the harvest. How long will you slumber, O sluggard? When will you rise from your sleep? A little sleep, a little slumber, A little folding of the hands to sleep so shall your poverty come on you like a prowler, and your need like an armed man." Proverbs is filled with commands against being time-wasters.   Proverbs 15:19, "The way of the lazy man is like a hedge of thorns, but the way of the upright is a highway." If Christians would only see the blessings which are just over the hill, they would always be time-redeemers.

For the believer, time is set aside by God. There are times of growth, times of blessing, times of trials, etc. God will order the times of every Christian to effectually bring about the sanctification they need. On the other hand, unbelievers try to take God's time and make it their own. They deliberately squander it because they think it is theirs to do with what they please. If they do not redeem the time they agree with the evil of the day and do not walk circumspectly and do not care for the commands of God. This is a fool, not walking as one who is wise. All the duties that you find in previous chapters concerning biblical reformation will only be taken seriously by one who redeems the time for Christ and His Kingdom. One will not be a good Christian, a good husband or wife, a good sibling, a good master or servant, without redeeming the time. Every opportunity to make the most of our time is taken.

"How to redeem the time" begins with redeeming the time through self-examination. Redeeming the time does not simply mean you use your time in a right way, though that is part of it. Time-redeemers "buy up the opportunity". The Christian views this life as a great opportunity. They are always thinking, "How might I please Christ my Lord in this opportunity, or in that?" The evaluation of every situation is of utmost importance and the Christian is to make the most of it. Non-Christians view this life differently. They make the most of this life for themselves. They settle down, marry, create wealth, etc. Their motto is, "Eat, drink and be merry for tomorrow we die." They are, in this, most foolish. They are not even as keen as the devil is. Even *Satan* redeems the time. The Scripture says in Luke 4:13, "Now when the devil had ended every temptation, he departed from Him until an opportune time." Even the devil will use time to his advantage and come at a "more opportune" time to destroy the works of God in His people – or at least attempt to do so. Satan is out to stop true biblical reformation from ever taking place. With the wicked, his job is easy because they are already walking zombies who care about only fulfilling their own desires. But for the Christian, Satan is out to ravage and destroy them so that reformation never occurs. Paul knew this. This is why Ephesians chapter six is given over to fighting heavenly battles by living out, wisely, the Word of God.

Ponder all the opportunities that you have lost and gained. Live your life as if you only had three days left to live; or less. Do you think such a man would strive to effectuate true biblical reformation at least for that time? Would he not make the most of it? Would you? Do you? Without redeeming the time, true biblical reformation will remain a Christian theory. It will never be put into practice.

"The heart in man is the first mover of the actions of man, even as the first mover carrieth all the spheres of heaven about with it; so doth this little thing in the little world of man, animate all his operations."

- Rev. Oliver Heywood, Heart Treasure

"A purification is not enough; a transformation is wanted."

- Guillermo Farel, Reformer with John Calvin in Geneva

❧ 12 ❧
Resolving to Guard the Heart

Proverbs 4:23, "Keep your heart with all diligence, For out of it spring the issues of life."

In dealing with "Biblical Reformation" Christians must know what true biblical reformation really is all about. Recapping what has been said in the previous chapters, first, true biblical reformation is only accomplished through the Word of God. Second, true biblical reformation is always joined to a solemn resolve to continue to follow God's Word. Third, true biblical reformation is always a thorough reform. These three principles are to be set within every context of the Christian life. Everything that envelops and involves the renewed Christian mind striving to become all that Christ desires us to be will overflow into the desire to continue true biblical reformation while the Christian dwells on this earth.

Not only should Christians be reminded of the principle of true biblical reformation, but they must know the various areas that Reformation should permeate. True biblical reformation should permeate the Church and its worship, the Offices of the church and the congregation of the church, the Home in every aspect which includes the federal husband, the industrious wife and the relationship between parents and children, and it should extent to the workplace in the relationship between employers and employees.

Also, Christians must make the most of every opportunity that is allotted for true biblical reformation to take place. Without walking circumspectly and wisely during the time they have here on earth, true biblical reformation will never occur.

Finally, there must be a discussion on having a practical outworking as to how all these things come to pass, and that practical outworking will only be accomplished by the armor of the Word of God kept safe in the heart. Keeping the heart of the Christian safe and sound from every intruder and everything that would steal away the Word which effectuates true biblical reformation is of prime importance. Why? The Christian may know what to do, but without protecting the Word of God in their heart, what they should do and what they accomplish are very different things. One is practical knowledge, the other is knowledge put into practice.

Proverbs 4:23 is set in the greater context of the admonition of keeping to the right path. One can resolve to walk a certain path and have good intentions, but practically, there is a way to go about making those resolutions come to pass. Proverbs 4:10-27 in its full context envelops the larger idea of various anatomical exhortations. There is a theology of walking set upon a right path. The eyes are mentioned in verses 21 and 25. The mouth is mentioned in verse 24. The feet are mentioned in verses 26 and 27. The right path is seen and walked, but it is by determination that it takes places. One path is light, the other is darkness. Proverbs 4:23, then, is crucial to taking the right path, for where the heart is, the body follows.

The proverb begins with the word "keep". It is the Hebrew word *natsar* which means "to watch, guard, keep". It also may mean "to preserve", "observe", "guard with fidelity" and to create a "blockaded". What is to be "kept" or "blockaded?" The text that says one should keep the "heart...", or even more literally, "your heart." The Hebrew here means "the inner man, mind, will and understanding "which also stands in conjunction with the "inclination, resolution, and determination of the will." This is effectively the idea for the soul. The heart is the center or seat of man's being. It knows (Proverbs 14:10, "The heart knows its own bitterness."). It has wisdom (Proverbs 14:33, "Wisdom rests in the heart of him who has understanding.") It is fallen and holds corruption (Jeremiah 17:9, "The heart is deceitful above all things, and desperately wicked; who can know it?") It thinks (Matthew 15:19, "For out of the heart proceed evil thoughts.") It is the seat of belief (Romans 10:10, "For with the heart one believes unto righteousness...."). And in the verse at hand, it is the center of resolve. This is much like what Christ says in Matthew 6:21, "For where your treasure is, there your heart will be also." As the heart is either pure or wicked, so is the whole course of a man's life.

How is one to "keep the heart?" The text reads "...with all diligence..." The Hebrew idea here is that it is the *mishmar* or "place of confinement." This is much like the idea of a prison, or a guard at a jail who has a guarded post where he watches and observes the prisoners very carefully. Literally this phrase translates, "As a guard watches the prisoner." As the guard watches and keeps the prisoner in jail, so also the Christian is to keep or guard the heart with a diligence or resolve the same as confining criminals. The Christian heart is like the lockdown procedure in a maximum security prison. What kind of thought and determination goes into how to hold criminals in such a foolproof facility? More thought should go into keeping the Christian heart safe from the world, flesh and devil.

The heart is to be kept because, "out of it spring the issues of life." Out of the heart comes forth everything that pertains to a man's path – all things regarding the manner and way of life. It is the place where life springs forth and defines the manner in which men live. It is, then, a crucial task to keep the heart safe and secure.

What the Text Teaches Us About Keeping Our Heart Safe

For True Biblical Reformation to take place, the Christian must *continually* protect his heart from that which may corrupt it. What is worth protecting? Guarding the heart is something that is set over the entire life of the Christian. It is not that just at certain times the heart should be guarded, but rather, it is protected all the time since the issues of life spring out of it. Those "issues" occur all through life, not just at certain times. Banks have elaborate safes to protect money. Homes have alarm systems to protect valuables. People have insurance policies to protect their families. What protects the heart? Christians are commanded to protect the heart with all diligence, like a guard over a prisoner, but how is that done? How is walking the right path accomplished?

Psalm 119:11 says, "Your word I have hidden in my heart, that I might not sin against You!" Ephesians 5:17 says, "Therefore do not be unwise, but understand what the will of the Lord is." Rev. John Flavel in his work *A Saint Indeed* says, "The keeping and right managing of the heart in every condition is the great business of a Christian's life"[1] Holding fast to the Word, and its memorization and incorporation is what sets the Christian on the Rock of Christ. Christ is the Living Logos - the

---

[1] John Flavel, *Works of Flavel*, Volume X, (Carlisle, Banner of truth Trust: 1995) 3.

Living Word. The Word of God, then, is hiding Christ in the heart for protection against the onslaught of the world, flesh and devil. God's Word is always under attack by the enemy. Genesis 3:1 records, "Now the serpent was more cunning than any beast of the field which the LORD God had made. And he said to the woman, "Has God indeed said, 'You shall not eat of every tree of the garden'?"" Zechariah 3:1 says, "Then he showed me Joshua the high priest standing before the Angel of the LORD, and Satan standing at his right hand to oppose him." 2 Corinthians 11:14 says, "And no wonder! For Satan himself transforms himself into an angel of light." Revelation 2:9 states that some were of the, "...synagogue of Satan." If the Word of God is set in the heart of a Christian, it will be a place of war. Satan, the world and the flesh will fight against the Word of God that is set in the Christian heart. They always have and always will until the end of the age. Guarding the heart is not easy work, and yet, it is *constant* work.

The heart should be guarded by principle. Psalm 4:4 says, "Be angry, and do not sin. Meditate within your heart on your bed, and be still. Selah." Psalm 77:6 says, "I call to remembrance my song in the night; I meditate within my heart, and my spirit makes diligent search."

The heart should also be guarded because of varying providences. Providences that befall the Christian are of different kinds. Each kind presents the manner in which the heart should be guarded. Prosperity may be a good thing. But the heart must be guarded even in good times. Psalm 62:10 says, "If riches increase, do not set your heart on them". Adversity can be hard. But the heart must be guarded. Proverbs 24:10 says, "If you faint in the day of adversity, your strength is weak." Guarding the heart in every circumstance creates consistency. Ecclesiastes 7:14 teaches, "In the day of prosperity be joyful, but in the day of adversity consider: Surely God has appointed the one as well as the other, so that man can find out nothing that will come after him." The heart should be guarded because of temptations of all kinds. Acts 5:3 record the sin of Ananias, "But Peter said, "Ananias, why has Satan filled your heart to lie to the Holy Spirit and keep back part of the price of the land for yourself?" Hosea 13:6 records the sin of Israel, "When they had pasture, they were filled; they were filled and their heart was exalted; Therefore they forgot Me." In every area, in every circumstance, the heart must be guarded and kept pure. It should be so fortified and have such a strong blockade of Scripture around it that it could withstand against the *possibility* of any temptation. It should be likened to the work of Nehemiah in Nehemiah 4:18, "Every one of the builders had his sword girded at his side as he built." Nehemiah's men building the wall did not stop. They had their sword and their trowel. They worked, and were prepared for battle.

At what point can a Christian stop keeping his heart? There is hardship all around in this fallen world. Out of the heart, comes the Christian's witness, and that witness must be constant. The Christian witness and testimony before men will be demonstrated by the holiness of the heart, or the lack of it. An unkept bed is distinguishable from a kept bed. If the heart is not kept – it will lack grace, it will lack giftedness, it will lack usefulness, it will lack assurance of salvation. What kind of witness a person has demonstrates in this regard the question as to how one keeps or not keeps their heart diligently for Christ.

Overall, the best remedy for an unguarded heart is to come to a greater knowledge of God. Knowing God more guards the heart. Many times there seems to be intricate lessons to learn from various Scriptures on different subjects for the Christian's edification. Those intricate outlines that sometimes seem to exhaust a subject can be very edifying, and some of the best sermonizing done. But the best remedy for a slack heart, is simply to get to know Christ more intimately, and God more exhaustively. The most neglected topic in theology is the Doctrine of God, and that is why most of the heresy that ruins the church falls around a *misapprehension* of *who* God is and *what* He is like. How would the Christian act differently about the nature of his heart, and it sanctification, or lack of it, if he were more intimately aware of the presence, holiness and character of God in their life? Guarding the heart is hard. Imagine how much more solemn it would be, and easier it would be if Christians had a more intimate knowledge of Christ's real presence with them? Think of it, God is constantly recording the thoughts of the Christian – all their actions, feelings, desires, intents, etc. Under the realization of a constant "Divine Scrutiny", the heart should be well guarded! Psalm 139:23 says, "Search me, O God, and know my heart; Try me, and know my anxieties." God is no doubt capable. Psalm 44:21 says, "Would not God search this out? for He knows the secrets of the heart." Jeremiah 17:10 makes the point vivid, "I, the LORD, search the heart, I test the mind, Even to give every man according to his ways, According to the fruit of his doings." And it should be a great scare, and a humble thought, to be reminded that everything will come into the Judgment. Matthew 12:36-37 says, "But I say to you that for every idle word men may speak, they will give account of it in the Day of Judgment. For by your words you will be justified, and by your words you will be condemned."" Christ's realized presence would make all the difference in keeping the heart faithfully.

Each time Christ appeared in His power to men, and they realized who He was, they coward. Luke 5:8 record the cowering of Peter in the boat with Christ when Peter said, "Depart from me, for I am a sinful man, O Lord!" John the Apostle in Revelation 1:17 said, "And when I saw Him, I fell at His feet as dead." The prophet Ezekiel in Ezekiel 1:28 says, "This was the appearance of the likeness of the glory of the LORD. So when I saw it, I fell on my face..." Truly, the study and meditation on the Doctrine of God would be a sure remedy for a heart that is not guarded, to become more guarded. To know God more intimately would spark a true reform in the life of the Christian.

How the Text Applies to Us in Reforming Our Hearts

Guarding our heart is the constant business of our lives. Without guarding our heart, true biblical reformation, and our dedication to it, would *never* occur. Continually guarding our heart first glorifies God in our confirmation of Christ's Image. We must never stop guarding our hearts in this manner. In this, we must keep ourselves from sin. Romans 8:13 bids us, "For if ye live after the flesh, ye shall die: but if ye through the Spirit do mortify the deeds of the body, ye shall live." Colossians 3:5 exhorts us, "Mortify therefore your members which are upon the earth; fornication, uncleanness, inordinate affection, evil concupiscence, and covetousness, which is idolatry." We are admonished in John 7:38, "He who believes in Me, as the Scripture has said, out of his heart will flow rivers of living water." And we are pressed to flee to Christ who, as 2 Corinthians 4:4 states, is "the light of the gospel of the glory of Christ, who is the image of God." Holiness is essential to success. But not just holiness one time enacted; rather holiness always pursued. If our minds are not wrapped around the concept of separation from the world and a separation and cleaving to God, then guarding the heart, or watching over it, will make little sense.

We must have a knowledge of the Word which is essential to success. This must be a continued, and it must never let up. The Genevan Reformer, Dr. Francis Turretin, was a master theologian and exegete. Any theologian today would do well to study Turretin and his works. He is my favorite of all theologians to study. He brought great prosperity to Geneva after John Calvin and Theodore Beza died. But, when his son took his place after his own death, Alphonses turned Geneva around, and sent it back into the hell it came from. The apostasy of Turretin's son was baffling, while at the same time exceedingly sad. Alphonses did not guard his heart. He did not walk circumspectly. He was not wise, and not diligent to glorify God in everything. Instead, he turned away and caused the people to follow idols. He did not desire true biblical reformation like his father before him.

If we desire true biblical Reformation in our home, work, church and society, then guarding our heart and keeping our hearts in the orthodoxy of the Word of God is of prime importance. People say doctrine is not important. Or sometimes, "too much doctrine is too much." This is the heckling of a fallen heart at the Word of God. Becoming more like Christ is only accomplished through the Word and we can never be enough in the Word or know the Word enough. If you corrupt the Word, or the proper use of the Word, then you corrupt the only means by which the Spirit sanctifies the soul. That is why Josiah tore his clothes after reading the book of the Law. He knew what they had lacked and how apostate they had become.

Without keeping our hearts safe, they will be restless to sin. Augustine said, "The soul is restless until it finds its rest in thee." How will the heart or soul ever be ready for sanctification without its keeping? How will it ever endure a time of trial or mission if it is not properly kept? Personal and Family devotions, church attendance, the use of personal gifts for the edification of the body, and all other like sanctifying works are essential to keeping the heart rightly.

God will not mold clay that is not set on the potter's wheel. All the success of true biblical reformation rests on whether or not the heart is set on the Word of God, and on Christ. Without this, true biblical reformation will never take place. You will then have knowledge of what is right, at the expense of doing what is right.

❧ 13 ❧
Gradual Reformation
Intolerable

A s we began, so we end. I brought to light the nature of biblical reformation under John Calvin in the introduction to
this short work. Here, I would like to remind the reader how
true biblical reformation played out in the history of the Reformation, and the nature or course that reformation took under
the guidance of able men such as Luther and Calvin. By com-
paring the nature of true biblical reformation in action, individual reformation in like manner may come to pass more readily. The reader should beware – gradual reformation is always
intolerable to those who love the Word of God, and strive to
uphold that Word in the life of the church, family and individual before Jesus Christ. Thus, is a gradual reformation intolerable to you?

The European Reformation embodies the biblical guide to
the nature of true reform and the convictions needful towards
an authentic transformation of a corrupt church into a holy
body. This will be proven in a moment. The notion, then, of a

gradual Reformation is at best *intolerable*. The saints of God should never settle for a "gradual reformation." Josiah, when confronted with the Law of God made radical changes in the *cultus* of Israel. In like manner, Martin Luther and John Calvin vigorously contended for the Reformation of the church, not a gradual accommodation in hopes of reform. It is true that the Reformers did not desire schism from the corrupt church. Rather, they desired to instill truth into it and recapture the virtue that had been lost under a cloak of spiritual degeneracy. Yet, after true biblical reformation had begun, the Roman Catholic Church could not accept such changes. The reformers knew that such changes would ultimately force the Protestants to break from the Roman Catholic Church in order to reestablish the virtues of biblical Christianity. In this way, it is impossible to deny that after the biblical Gospel settled in the hands of converted reformers, pastors and theologians of that day (as in previous biblical days) that true Reformation progressed through impositions upon certain immediate and necessary obligations in relation to ecclesiology (the regulative principle of worship and church discipline) and Sacramentology (the right administration of the sacraments). In other words, the nature of the argument set forth in chapter 4 about worship is not something that the church should gradually work its way into. Rather, as God has so commanded His people, they should obey. It is the same as with lying. If a man is a compulsive liar, should he gradually change or should be repent of his lying? Would it be acceptable to God to lie a little, and gradually change, or does require men to repent of their sin?

In the 2007 movie "Amazing Grace", William Wilberforce is shown over his 15 year attempt at abolishing slavery in England. The slave trade had grown so wicked, that freighting ships would take on more salves in their hulls than they were allowed by double the amount, and over 600 of 800 slaves would die on the journey home. While recounting all the horrific statistics of these trade ships, Wilberforce attempted time and time again over that 15 year span, to have Parliament abolish slavery. One man, teetering on a dubious middle position, stood up and agreed with Wilberforce that slavery should be abolished, but only gradually. How does one take into account the atrocities of the slave trade and desire to "gradually" put an end to it? In the same way and manner God is not pleased with a "gradual reformation" of the essential truths of the bible, but a thorough reform like the one Josiah enacted in his day.

Gradual reformation has never been the matrix in which the church has functioned since its inception in the Garden of Eden. Yet, various New Testament epistles embrace a tenderness in which reformation should be accomplished, and in some instances, elementary doctrines should be taught again (e.g. Hebrews 5:12-14). It is a tragedy that churches, at various points in their spirituality, cannot bear to hear certain doctrines or ideas lest they become overwhelmed because of their inadequacy in understanding the Bible. Nonetheless, in beginning to teach elementary doctrines again, this does not infer that the foundations of basic principles be abandoned in order to accommodate the people of God in their waywardness. It is the opinion of the reformers that a context for teaching biblically sound doctrine is only found in a church that desires to lay the principles of a biblical reformation down first, and then advance in biblical teaching from those basic fundamental maxims.

Let us recap the basic definition of what it means to reform something. "Reformation" is defined by Webster's Dictionary as "a 16th century *religious movement* marked ultimately by *rejection* or *modification* of some Roman Catholic doctrine and practice and establishment of the Protestant churches."[1] It is

---

[1] Emphasis mine.

the state of being "reformed." To be "reformed" or to "reform" means, "1a) to put or change into an improved form or condition 1b) to amend or improve by change of form or removal of faults or abuses 2) *to put an end to an evil by enforcing or introducing a better method or course of action*, 3) to induce or *cause to abandon* evil ways."[2] Reformation, then, confronts and changes the *status quo* in order to improve, amend, and introduce a better method of procedure (in this case – the sanctification of the Christian). It removes, puts an end to, and abandons false or evil ways that hinder that which should already be in place. In terms of *the* Reformation, it is the abandonment and repudiation of evil or wicked devices of men instituted in the church through false doctrines, and to establish, change and amend those ways by immediate interposition of improved change to the foundations of ecclesiastical truth found in Scripture. That is a mouthful! In simpler terminology - it is a formal return to sound doctrine and truth previously eclipsed by sin and ignorance – and it was not accomplished gradually.

Martin Luther and True Biblical Reformation

In considering the biblical actions of Martin Luther in Germany, we find an instantaneous imposition of reform once Luther embraces the truth of the Word of God. Luther was converted, became a priest, went to Rome, and upon his return within 2 years, set the *95 Theses* in motion. Yet, even before this, being a learned Doctor of Theology, his fame was spreading through Europe attracting students from every nearby country. Scholastic philosophy and theological methods had been undermined, and a *via moderna* (a new and modern way) of yet another sort stood in its place. Just as Jesus began his public ministry with the expulsion of the profane traffickers from the court of the temple (John 2:14ff), so Luther began his

---

[2] Emphasis mine.

ministry by preaching and lecturing against relics and indulgences – a desire to rid the Roman Church of its abuses against
the people of God. The official statement to this did not come
long afterwards, but relatively quickly in the 95 *Theses*.

The Reformation began with a public protest against the
traffic of indulgences that profaned and degraded the Christian
religion.[3]   Phillip Schaff writes, "After serious deliberation,
without consulting any of his colleagues or friends, but following an irresistible impulse, Luther resolved upon a public act of
unforeseen consequences."[4] Luther's desire was not to break
off from the church under these reforms, but to debate in the
accepted manner of scholasticism on the questions raised by his
95 *Theses* against indulgences. At first, Pope Leo X did not
bother with the *Theses* believing it was simply the ravings of a
drunken monk whose influence would soon dissipate.   But
when Luther's "reforms" began to reach into the pocket of the
Pope, Leo wanted him silenced. The fact that such a document
was made public, and pinned on a church door, attests that this
crucial move was not one done in secret. There were no pre-
tences in Luther's actions at all. Reformation makes men bold
in God's power and grace.

What was Luther's response to Rome's desire for him to
stop preaching the truth after the *Theses* was published? With
the "stroke of an axe" the Reformation began, but was there a
lapse in its continuation?   Luther's mind was bound to the
Word of God and unless one could convince him of his errors
by its authority, he would not change his course. Even the *Theses* read, "I implore all men, by the faith of Christ, either to
point out to me a better way, if such a way has been divinely
revealed to any, or at least to submit their opinion to the judg-

---

[3] Phillip Schaff, *History of the Christian Church*, Volume 7, Grand Rapids, MI,
1994. Page 118.
[4] Martin Luther's 95 *Thesis*, Ages Software, 2000.

ment of God and of the Church."[5] In attempting to silence Luther, Pope Leo had Prierias write a "crushing blow" against the
Theses in Latin. Luther replied, and then Prierias replied back
again. The correspondence simply widened the breach already
begun by Luther. Yet, even while this correspondence was occurring, Rome had already decided to brand Luther as a heretic, and commanded him to appear in Rome within sixty days to
recant his heresies. Luther met with the cordial Cajetan three
times. Cajetan attempted to dissuade Luther, through a cordial
friendship, and demanded of him strict allegiance to the Pope
and a retraction of his errors. Upon his last meeting, Cajetan
threatened him with excommunication having already the papal mandate in his hand, and dismissed him with the words,
"Revoke, or do not come again into my presence."[6] Luther did
not bend. Rather, he escaped that night and rode back to Wittenberg. Is this the ploy of *gradual* Reformation?

Before being called to the Diet of Worms, another attempt
was made to silence Luther when Pope Leo sent Karl von Miltitz to meet with him in order to, affably, aid him in recanting
his heresy. After the meeting, Miltitz seemed to believe he
made headway with Luther, yet Luther would not think of recanting his ideas. Luther did write a humble letter to the Pope
expressing his desire to reform the church, but not to recant his
ideas. At the same time, Pope Leo had a papal bull drawn up
which demanded his recantation, or his excommunication and
death. Luther's response to this was a public gathering of students and faculty at Wittenberg to witness the burning of the
papal bull, upon reception of it. The implementations of these
acts do not lend itself to a gradual reformation, but a Reformation that imposed restriction and reaction against false doc-

---

[5] Phillip Schaff, *History of the Christian Church*, Volume 7, Grand Rapids, MI,
1994. Page 32.
[6] Schaff, 35.

trine. In no way, and at no time, could Luther go back to the
false doctrine that he had been raised upon as a monk just to
appease the consciences of men. Gradual Reformation in any
way is intolerable to the truth, as it was to Luther who stood
upon the Word. The doctrines of grace and justification were
planted in the heart of the Reformer and could not be removed.
Reformation was based on these *convictions* brought about *by
the Word of God.* Miller says, "Henceforth the doctrine of justification by faith alone was for him to the end of life the sum and
substance of the gospel, the heart of theology, the central truth
of Christianity, the article of the standing or falling church."[7]

Knowing Luther had not yet recanted, a Diet was called by
Charles V (where Pope Leo X was represented) where Luther
was summoned to Wittenberg. He was asked two questions in
which he would reply in German and Latin – 1) Are these your
writings? and, 2) Will you recant them? Luther asked for time
in which to gather his thoughts and give a reply. Some would
say this desire is exemplary of a "gradual reformation," however, the night was spent in prayer in order to answer them in a
manner in which would be glorifying to God.[8] Luther had no
intentions of recanting. Schaff says, "On the same evening Luther recollected himself, and wrote to a friend: I shall not re-
tract one iota, so Christ help me."[9] Upon the next day these
questions were placed on him again. His answer is the epitome
of a rejection of gradual reformation, "Unless I am refuted and
convicted by testimonies of the Scriptures or by clear arguments (since I believe neither the Pope nor the Councils alone;
it being evident that they have often erred and contradicted
themselves), I am conquered by the Holy Scriptures quoted by

---

[7] Arthur Miller, *Miller's Church History*, (Ages software, 2000), 104.
[8] See d'Aubigne's *History of the Reformation in the 16th Century* for Luther's prayer
that night.
[9] Schaff, 53.

me, and my conscience is bound to the word of God: I can not and will not recant any thing, since it is unsafe and dangerous to do any thing against the conscience." If Luther really desired to "win their affections" and appease their consciences, he could have thrown aside the Scriptures and simply bowed down to Emperor Charles V. Instead his recapitulation of Christ's words, "If I have spoken evil, bear witness of me," testifies to his solidity toward reforming the church through the washing of the Word of God.

After the doctrinal break made with Rome the German Reformation could not be stopped. It was excessive in terms of those "being reformed" but its excessive character is not surprising. Staupitz, Luther's father of monkery, held fast to the unity of the Roman Catholic Church and was intimidated and repelled by the *excesses* of the Reformation.[10] The Pope issued a papal bull against Luther. Delegates were sent to him in order to silence him. His former mentors were encouraged to dissuade him. John Eck, the renowned Roman Catholic theologian debated his "heresies." A Diet led by the Emperor called him to recant. In all this Luther remained steadfast upon the Word of God. At this point, the Reformation for Luther did not slow down, but increased. He debated the Swiss reformer Ulrich Zwingli on the meaning and sacramentology of the Lord's Supper, completed a New Testament translation in German, wrote vehemently against the abuses of the Roman Catholic Church, and wrote voluminously for the edification of the Protestant Church. Luther's Reformation was anything but gradual. Many of his reforms were reactionary and instilled overnight. It is historically impossible to call the reforms of the German church throughout Luther's day anything but "excessive," and the opposite of a "gradual and subtle Reformation." In this way, the reader must come to grips in noticing the same move-

---

[10] Schaff, 102.

ments that Luther made mimicked the work of Josiah in the days of Israel. Reformation is according to the Word of God, complete and covenanted by oath to the truth of the Word.

John Calvin and True Biblical Reformation

In the Swiss Reformation the writings of John Calvin are preeminent, and the work of Calvin in his tract *The Necessity of Reforming the Church* is the best treatment explaining his rejection of a gradual reformation over an actual *true biblical Reformation*. His work is readily accessible, and clearly articulates the grievances of overthrowing or hindering an actual Reformation from taking place.

Calvin's work in Geneva is exemplary of true biblical Reformation. Certainly there were extremes that should be avoided (such as the State's physical persecution of the Anabaptists, the consent to the burning of Servetus, and the abusive imprisonments against the Genevans themselves). Yet, even in avoiding the extremes, the Genevan model of Reformation coincides with the same foundation as the German Reformation did for Luther –once the Word of God is implemented, true biblical change (reformation) is inevitable. The reader is reminded of his tract from the introduction. Calvin wanted to see true biblical reform take place so that the Regulative Principle of the Church would not be displaced. This was not something he wanted to see gradually take place over a period of fifty years, but something, based on the Word of God, that should take place right now.

Why is Calvin so adamant to press immediate reform instead of gradual reform? Every area of worship that is overthrown by the devices of men becomes void of worship to God's holy commandments. For instance, the Lord's Supper had been violently corrupted by the mass in Calvin's day, and turned into a "theatrical exhibition."[11] It was resembled more by magical arts (sacerdotalism), rather than testifying to the significance and truth of the Supper. It ceased to be worship, and became an exercise in futility – much like the estranged view of Zwingli's memorialism in his view of the Lord's Supper.

What are the remedies to overthrow sin within the church? According to Calvin, there must be an immediate return to the legitimate worship of God and the ground of salvation. In Calvin's day this would mean the expulsion of everything in "worship" not prescribed in the Bible by good and necessary inference or by the direct institution of God – no idolatry, prayers to the saints, transubstantiation, vestments, and the like. The Word of God should regulate worship, the sacraments were to be administered rightly, and the government of the church should be set in order.

After setting forth the evils and the remedies to those evils concerning false worship, Calvin then pleads for "Reformation required without delay."[12] Though many would have desired to see Calvin silenced on these issues since they were creating a tumultuous season for the church, Calvin defends himself by demonstrating that such a peace devoid of reform is really a false peace, and a cloak that covers evil. And to rail against Calvin and the other reformers such as Luther (whom Calvin mentions in the work), is really to rail against God himself since these reformers were simply following the Scriptures and the warrants set therein. Calvin says, "In a corruption of sound doctrine so extreme, in a pollution of the sacraments so nefarious, in a condition of the Church so deplorable, those who maintain that we ought not to have felt so strongly, would have been satisfied with nothing less than a perfidious tolerance, by which we should have betrayed the worship of God, the glory of Chr-

---

[11] Calvin, *The Necessity of Reforming the Church*, 29.
[12] Calvin, 88.

ist, the salvation of men, the entire administration of the sacraments, and the government of the Church. There is something specious in the name of moderation, and tolerance is a quality which has a fair appearance, and seems worthy of praise; but the rule which we must observe at all hazards is, never to endure patiently that the sacred name of God should be assailed with impious blasphemy — that his eternal truth should be suppressed by the devil's lies — that Christ should be insulted, his holy mysteries polluted, unhappy souls cruelly murdered, and the Church left to writhe in extremity under the effect of a deadly wound. This would be not meekness, but indifference about things to which all others ought to be postponed."[13] Such deceitful and disloyalty to the Word of God, and subsequently God himself, cannot be tolerated. Exacting the rightful administration of church discipline upon matters that deviate from the Word of God is most necessary. To have right worship prescribed by the Word, a right administration of the sacraments, and a right exercise of church discipline, are, as this tract vividly portrays, the marks of a *true* church.

In demonstrating the intentions behind Calvin's Genevan reforms and the necessity of their instantaneous administration, as well as seeing, by example, the actions of Martin Luther filled with doctrinal zeal, can Christians imitate these men on sure ground that they acted biblically?   Christian practices should consistently be guided by the principles of the Word of God. Is there evidence in the Word of God for laying an immediate foundation of biblical principles in the church as opposed to a long gradual reform? Did Luther and Calvin follow the Bible on this? To answer this question the following biblical texts speak to the issue: Lev. 10:3; 1 Samuel 15:22, Matthew 15:9, Col. 2:23; 2 Chron. 14:4 (cf. 1 Kings 15:3); 2 Chron. 29:1; 2 Kings 22:1ff; John 2:12ff.

---

[13] Calvin, 107-108.

Regulating Life by God's Principles

  Lev. 10:3, 1 Samuel 15:22 and Matthew 15:9 set the standard and basis for the Regulative Principle of worship defined by Calvin above. Calvin goes to great lengths to prove this. Luther contested for the Word in this manner and the direction of the Word in every area of the church – which is why the Pope, Cardinals, and theologians of the Catholic Church were so irate with him (he placed the Word above everything and subsequently removed their power). Leviticus 10:3 demonstrates the sanctity of God's mind in worship, "And Moses said to Aaron, "This is what the LORD spoke, saying: 'By those who come near Me I must be regarded as holy; And before all the people I must be glorified.' "So Aaron held his peace." Here we see that the worshipper will sanctify the Lord in his worship to Him, or God will sanctify Himself in judgment against the worshipper (as Nadab and Abihu had been killed by God for offering strange fire). 1 Samuel 15:22 says, "Then Samuel said: "Has the LORD as great delight in burnt offerings and sacrifices, as in obeying the voice of the LORD? Behold, to obey is better than sacrifice, And to heed than the fat of rams." In this instance Saul had taken it upon himself to do what he wanted in worshipping God without the sanction of God or the help of Samuel, and so the rebuke is given – God disdains self-imposed worship offered up by selfish hearts. And Matthew 15:9 states, "And in vain they worship Me, Teaching as doctrines the commandments of men." Here the Lord Jesus explains that men will replace the true worship of the church with that which is expedient or satisfying for themselves. Jesus teaches that such worship leads to vanity, i.e. it is waste of time, and brings condemnation. God must be sanctified in worship (set apart and regarded as holy, honored with a right heart and right sacrifices, and worshipped in the context of His prescriptions of worship) not the vain self-flattery of a man made will worship.

Calvin spent a great amount of time working through Colossians 2:23a, "Which things have indeed a shew of wisdom in will worship..." To remind the reader once again, "will worship" is that which is fabricated and implemented in the stead of true worship. It is devised by men, and hinders communion with God. It may have a show of wisdom (i.e. people participating in it may think it is quite good and helpful) but in the end it simply tears people away from Christ and leads them astray. It is false worship, and causes a rift between the worshipper and the Lord. Experience does not dictate worship, or the forms of worship. Rather, the Word of God is the only rule by which worship is defined by what God commands and sanctions. Any attempt at addition or subtraction to His Word is done at the peril of men's souls.

Luther's mind was set ablaze when he understood the grace of God. He could not contain himself. He was thrust forth over a series of providences that pressed him ever forward towards the Reformation of the church. Calvin's defense of his actions, or all the actions of the Reformers, is based on the urgency of adhering to the Scriptural warrants for worship. If anything else is substituted or taken away, then true worship cannot be obtained. In this respect, the question must be asked of today's theologians, pastors and laymen, "Do the Scriptures warrant an immediate change or a gradual change in the Reformation of the church?" Calvin and Luther opted for an *immediate* change. Though the Scriptures command reform, and constitute that which is right for worship, do they also demonstrate the time in which reformation should take place? The answer is a resounding "yes." The Old Testament and the New Testament abound with examples of instant reform in the church bringing the people back to a right worship of God. The reader could recall chapter 1!

Most of the kings of Israel and Judah (God's "anointed" leaders) did not follow His Word. They implemented false worship to foreign gods for personal or national expediency. Some kings brought the people back to biblical worship. Time could be spent with the partial reform of Asa (though partial reform, even if it is enacted immediately, is never ultimately beneficial. (cf. 2 Chronicles 14:4)). Better lessons can be gleaned from the complete reforms of Hezekiah and obviously Josiah as outlined in the beginning of this book.

Hezekiah and Josiah demonstrated an *immediate* and *complete* reform over degenerated worship. Concerning Hezekiah, 2 Chronicles 29:2-3 says, "And he did that which was right in the sight of the LORD, according to all that David his father had done. He in the first year of his reign, in the first month, opened the doors of the house of the LORD, and repaired them." He continued to restore true worship, which would degenerate after his death in the reign of Manasseh, one of the most wicked and ruthless kings of Israel. In verses 35-36 it says, "So the service of the house of the LORD was set in order. And Hezekiah rejoiced, and all the people, that God had prepared the people: for the thing was done suddenly." The Hebrew word *pithowm* for "done suddenly" means "suddenly or surprisingly." This cleansing of the temple and restoration of true worship was done "at once." It was "unexpected" by the people, so to speak. It is clear that Hezekiah had the complete restoration of worship in mind, not by gradual means, but with immediacy, and according to the Word of God.

By way of reminder once again, Josiah was no different. Briefly - Josiah's account in the Biblical record gleams with fervency in his restoration and reformation of worship. Israel's history here mirrors the darkness of the Roman Catholic reign and the rise of the Reformers. Manasseh and Amon had plunged the people into false worship, again. They were burning their children in the hands of Molech, and worshipping on the high places. Manasseh has the longest reign of any king, and he was the most wicked of them all. During his reign Baal was a household name. Amon was as wicked as Manasseh, his father, and the people of God continued to have a famine from the truth of the Word. Under their reigns, the Law of God was lost. After the death of Amon, Josiah rose to the throne and began to reign at 8 years old. Once he attained a mature age (eighteen) he reigned powerfully. He began a restoration of worship even before he had received the book of the Law that would have been discovered some 7 years later. After finding and reading the Law, 2 Kings 23:3-4 records the following, "And the king stood by a pillar, and made a covenant before the LORD, to walk after the LORD, and to keep his commandments and his testimonies and his statutes with all their heart and all their soul, to perform the words of this covenant that were written in this book. And all the people stood to the covenant. And the king commanded Hilkiah the high priest, and the priests of the second order, and the keepers of the door, to bring forth out of the temple of the LORD all the vessels that were made for Baal, and for the grove, and for all the host of heaven: and he burned them without Jerusalem in the fields of Kidron, and carried the ashes of them unto Bethel." The King had torn his robes and reinstated worship based on the book of the Law. He wasted no time and immediately restored the worship of God. He burned everything that desecrated the house of the Lord down at the river Kidron, and killed all the idolatrous priests who offered up worship to false gods. He crushed the statues of Molech, burned the chariots of the Sun, smashed every graven image into dust and destroyed all the altars that Ahaz had set up years earlier. He even burned the bones of dead men in the sepulchers because the people were worshipping them. Then, 2 Kings 23:22 records these words, "And the king commanded all the people, saying, Keep the Passover unto the LORD your God, as it is written in the book of this covenant." The key here is "as it is written in the book of the covenant." Josiah *immediately* and with *resolve* restored worship to its *biblical paradigm*. This is what Luther had done, and what Calvin had contended for in his polemic. This is true biblical reformation.

Jesus was no less zealous for the institution of God's true worship in His house than these righteous kings were - He was more so. As noted briefly at the beginning, Jesus began His public ministry by cleansing the temple. In John 2:14-17 we have this account, "And He found in the temple those who sold oxen and sheep and doves, and the moneychangers doing business. When He had made a whip of cords, He drove them all out of the temple, with the sheep and the oxen, and poured out the changers' money and overturned the tables. And He said to those who sold doves, "Take these things away! Do not make My Father's house a house of merchandise!" Then His disciples remembered that it was written, "Zeal for Your house has eaten Me up." The modern evangelical church would never have succumbed to this. They would have set up a booth next to the other vendors, become their friends, and would have attempted to win them to the "truth" over a course of time by identification. Jesus, on the other hand, drove these men out with a whip. Why the contrast? Christ had an unmitigated zeal for the truth of the Word and a desire to see true worship instituted (cf. John 4:24). Immediately Christ overturned the "accepted" manner of worship and merchandising in the temple, to demonstrate the zeal, or fervor of spirit, for the worship of God. Reformation for Christ was immediate, and used a strategy to overthrow the *status quo* by building a new church through his apostles alongside of the corrupt church. In the cleansing of the temple, we see a departure from the false status of worship, to a recreation of the full reality of worship in the church that

Christ came to build. Jesus had no time to waste, and in the course of three years taught his disciples to turn the world upside down, as Acts 17:6 says, "These that have turned the world upside down are come hither also."

For the modern church, and the modern Christian, there are many lessons to heed both from the Scriptures and the Reformers who implemented true biblical reformation. First, though more knowledge may flame more zeal and reform over time (as in the case with Luther) this does not mean the current evangelical knowledge obtained should lie dormant. Luther's Reformation was made up of a number of short bursts, or "little" reformations surrounding knowledge gained as he continued to study. As truths were made evident, they were implemented at all cost – even to his the peril of his own excommunication and death. To understand the truth surrounding any theological maxim, and to neglect imposing it in the life of the people, is sin (Rom. 14:23b; James 4:17). It should be agreed that prudence in implementation is necessary. But when the fundamentals of the faith are overthrown, and reformation surrounding those fundamentals are neglected though they be known by the Elders of the church, this is intolerable. If right worship, the right administration of the sacraments, and the exercise of biblical church discipline, are not set in the context of congregational life, it would be sin for the Elders to acquiesce to the congregation's theological ignorance. Implementation should be immediate.

Second, the Word of God is the only rule for faith and practice in the church where Jesus Christ is Head. *The Westminster Confession of Faith* says, "But the acceptable way of worshiping the true God is instituted by himself, and so limited by his own revealed will, that he may not be worshiped according to the imaginations and devices of men, or the suggestions of Satan, under any visible representation, or any other way not prescribed in the Holy Scripture."[14] This parallels Calvin's argument throughout the *Necessity of Reforming the Church*. To add or take away from prescribed worship is sin. Ministers who compromise this principle to uphold a some regular aspect of their own fabricated worship compromise the integrity of the Word and their own convictions. Christians who compromise the truth are hypocrites.

Thirdly, in speaking to Christian ministers, those elders who fail to reform their church by implementing the Scriptures upon the life of the congregation compromise their own beliefs. Worship then becomes man-centered rather than Christ-centered. If they truly believed the Word of God, then right worship would necessarily be implemented by compulsion to obey God rather than please men.

Fourthly, speaking again to ministers, such elders cannot be church leaders by way of pretence. If Calvin had gone to Geneva to slowly reform the church, reform would have never taken place. His preaching, teaching, and catechistical instruction would have been hindered at every turn. He would not have been able to speak plainly and openly about the truth. Ministers must clearly and precisely make their theological convictions known to a church before they enter into it. The church should know precisely what changes will occur the moment the pastor enters the church. Anything less than this would be sin, and the pastor would be there in pretence. He would be a liar. He would lie to God, for not believing His Word enough to instigate it. He would lie to himself, for thinking that he believed a set of theological truths, when in fact, he really does not – for belief constitutes implementation and trust in those truths. He would be lying to the congregation by facade demonstrating a fabrication of false intentions in order to gradually win them over to the "truth" later on. It is forgotten by many that the fa-

---

[14] *Westminster Confession of Faith* 21:1.

ther of lies is the devil. Such a position in terms of gradual reformation, is nothing but devilish wiles. If the Reformers had taken this position the Reformation would have never occurred. The Reformers would have died before they could have made any real implementations to the truth.

Fifthly, prudent reform takes place without the fear of men, and usually in the midst of contention. Luther and Calvin were consistently in the midst of conflict and difficulties due to the position they held to the truth. Recanting on revealed truth was not an option. Whenever sinful people are faced with the truth, disputation results. Such strife is impossible to avoid unless one compromises the truth. It may be after a long while that a congregation would mature in the truth, and such changes or implementations would be made more easily, but the historical record of the Bible and the Reformation do not support this. Sinful people hate godly change. Calvin and Farel were expelled from Geneva for preaching their convictions and standing on the Word of God! Likewise, the moneychangers in the temple were not happy that Jesus overturned their tables. The religious leaders sought to kill Christ at every turn! Instead, theological compromise hopes that "later on" the church will understand the foundations of the faith so that the basics of worship, the sacraments, and discipline may be enacted successfully.

It would be wise imitating Hezekiah, Josiah, Luther, Calvin and the Lord Jesus Christ in the achievement of immediate reformation. Compromise is a *lie*. True Biblical Reformation for both the church and the Christian is biblically necessary. Gradual reformation in this regard is *intolerable*. It is intolerable both for the people of God who are deceived as to what real reformation and truth are about, and to the minister who compromises his beliefs, and neglects the honor of God's desire in true spiritual worship to become man-pleasers. May it be that true biblical reformation would be the norm, and sanctification would radically change the face of the church all over the world for the glory of Christ. Pray that true biblical reformation would affect the church, the home, the workplace and all of society for the glory of the great King, Jesus Christ, and the Kingdom of God.

finis

You may obtain this and many other fine resources
published by Puritan Publications by contacting us:

Web:
www.puritanpublications.com

Email:
media@puritanpublications.com

Postal Mail:
Puritan Publications
834 Morgan Street
Elgin, Illinois 60123
United States of America

Puritan Publications is a ministry of A Puritan's Mind.
For an array of helpful online Reformed and Puritan
resources, please visit www.apuritansmind.com.

www.ingramcontent.com/pod-product-compliance
Lightning Source LLC
Chambersburg PA
CBHW020905100426
42737CB00043B/238